Three Ways Home

BOOKS BY

Sheila Kaye-Smith

————————————————

ROSE DEEPROSE

SUPERSTITION CORNER

GIPSY WAGGON

THE MIRROR OF THE MONTHS

SUMMER HOLIDAY

SUSAN SPRAY

SHEPHERDS IN SACKCLOTH

THE END OF THE HOUSE OF ALARD

JOANNA GODDEN

ISLE OF THORNS

SUSSEX GORSE

THREE AGAINST THE WORLD

THE TRAMPING METHODIST

THE CHALLENGE TO SIRIUS

STARBRACE

TAMARISK TOWN

SPELL LAND

LITTLE ENGLAND

GREEN APPLE HARVEST

THE GEORGE AND THE CROWN

JOANNA GODDEN MARRIED

THE VILLAGE DOCTOR

*

Three Ways Home

○ ○

An Experiment in Autobiography

by

Sheila Kaye-Smith

○ ○ ○ ○ ○ ○ ○ ○ ○ ○ ○ ○ ○ ○ ○ ○ ○ ○ ○ ○

HARPER & BROTHERS PUBLISHERS

New York *and* London

1937

THREE WAYS HOME

Contents

o o o

[v]

CONTENTS

Three Ways Home

Prologue in a Doctor's Brougham

MY FATHER's "pill-box" brougham is waiting outside a patient's house, and I am sitting in it and
watching the last of the November sunset—little
curls and feathers of burning cloud tossed over a
rainy green field above the smoking chimneys
of Hastings. I am about fifteen years old and I have,
according to a candid cousin, "a hideous grey
face." I do not mind—my face is nothing to me. I
have washed it this morning and will probably
(unless hard pressed) wash it again to-night, but
many years will pass before I take any more
trouble about it.

Perhaps my elders might have taken more
trouble; they might have decided, for instance, that
a little girl whose forehead amounts to almost half
her face would look better with a fringe. But I
don't think they cared any more than I did how
plain I was, and certainly I should have protested
if they had asked me to run counter to the fashions
of my school, which demanded hair skinned back
from the brows and plaited so tightly that the pig-

[1]

tail stood out almost at right-angles from the neck. They had concentrated their efforts on my clothes, and I wore a blouse which they had painstakingly covered with braid and buttons. School uniforms were many years ahead—I never wore one; but I wore a sailor hat with my school hat-band round it, bearing the arms of the borough of Hastings and the legend *Non Sine Pulvere Palma*.

I was waiting for my father to come out and drive me five miles into the country, to a house near Westfield where he had patients. It was now many years since he had given up his country practice, but a St. Leonards family who had left the town had contracted for his attendance, and I always went with him when he visited them—such a visit generally meaning tea and a delightful evening with people of my own age.

To-day for some reason the call was not to be made a social occasion. I cannot remember why it was so late; we did not often drive to Westfield in the dark, for the lanes were narrow and awkward, and the double journey by the light of carriage lamps could not be made in less than two hours. But though I had nothing to look forward to beyond the drive, this was happiness enough for me.

Merely to be in the country, to smell the grass and soil, to see the night sky brushing down over the fields, to hear the swish and murmur of the wind in the trees—all this was heart's delight, and always had been for as long as I could remember, and always would be, I had not the slightest doubt.

When I was grown up I would live by myself in the country, in a little cottage on the lane between Westfield and Sedlescome—I had already chosen it. I would also be a celebrated author, whose novels of rural life were famous throughout the world; and I would be extremely High Church—I should have no one to prevent me.

It is remarkable to think how I have stepped into this Eden, with only just those differences as real life imposes on a hectic imagination. I live in the country, though I do not live alone, and I should be extremely sorry to live in that little cottage; I have gained a certain reputation as a novelist of rural life, though it must inevitably fall short of the glory I imagined at fifteen; and as for being High Church, I am now a Roman Catholic, though I cannot be sure if this would have thrilled or appalled the schoolgirl in the brougham.

I can still see myself sitting there, deep in reflection. It is too dark to read, so I am thinking—an unfortunate pastime, I am to find, in later life, but safe enough now when I cannot put my thoughts on paper. I want to know exactly why I am so happy—it is not entirely because of the coming drive to Westfield; and I decide that it is for three reasons. My happiness comes from three things which are in particularly good case with me at the moment—the country, my writing and my religion. Not, perhaps, typical sources of bliss for a schoolgirl of fifteen. But for as long as I can remember these three things have made me happy. There was never a time when I did not know and love the country outside Hastings—Platnix and the primrose lane by Ireland Farm, where Father used to drive us as tiny children to fill our hands with flowers. Why, the first poem I ever made up was about Platnix:

> "O think of the two oast-houses,
> Up on yonder high . . ."

And now that the bicycle has enlarged my horizons I am writing a novel called *Northward of Brede*. It begins:

"The river Tillingham floweth out of the west and loses its waters in the silent Rother. On its way it passes many a gaunt farm-house with neglected pastures sloping down to the streamlet's bank, but never one more gaunt and neglected than Ellenwhorne."

(Can it be that my literary style has never changed since then?)

The country and my writing are really two different parts of the same thing. They are so interwoven that I cannot separate them. And as for religion, that is the third strand in the shining cord. When I was a little girl I thought that heaven was a hop-garden with roses growing up the poles instead of hops, and now at fifteen, though of course I no longer believe anything so childish, I find it difficult to picture a heaven which bears no relation to the country of Platnix and Northward of Brede. Short of seeing its beauties reflected in the Beatific Vision (as to this day I believe I must), I look forward to a heaven on earth, from which there shall be no drive back into the town . . . where I shall live and work and pray—very much as I am doing now in 1937.

I feel such an utterly different person from that schoolgirl that I find it hard to realize that my life is linked with hers by the faithful following out of her ambitions. Few people, I imagine, can be so logically connected with themselves at fifteen. I suppose that most people by the time they reach middle age have acquired an entirely new set of wishes and ideas, but mine are only an enlargement of those I started life with.

If to-day I had to decide what are the three best things in life I should want to make them four. The schoolgirl in the brougham seems strangely indifferent to human love, until you realize that in one respect (family and friends) she took it for granted and that in another (courtship and marriage) she had no use for it except in so far as it gives glamour to fiction. But the country, writing and religion still mean to me very much what they meant to her. Certainly they are just as closely woven together. I could not separate the religious thread from the others, to write what aims at being a religious autobiography, without quite destroying the pattern of my life.

So in giving the story of my progress towards the Catholic Church, I cannot ignore my progresses and retrogresses as an author, or the background which a certain small corner of England made for the combined action. It was indirectly through a novel of mine that I returned to the practice of religion, long before I actually became a Catholic; and a Sussex farm played an important part in my passage from the Church of England to the Church of Rome.

Of course, the story of any conversion could be written in two words—God's Grace. My aim here is not to account for my conversion, not even to make it appear reasonable, but simply to describe how actually that grace worked for *me*. For others it would no doubt work quite differently, so I do not expect any of my experiences to be convincing in themselves. My aim is not to present an argument for Catholicism, but simply to tell the tale of how I, personally, became a Catholic. I say this because so often the purpose of a book of this kind is misunderstood and automatically regarded as persuasion. If ever it is so it can be only in a secondary sense. The main story is psychological, and religious only in so far as it shows how God's grace works through and often in spite of man's mind, turning even its limitations to divine purposes.

My own impression is that one thing stands out clearly from it all, and that is that I have never really changed my religion. I have always been latently and potentially a Catholic—there has been no swing round from a contradictory set of ideas. I joined the Church of Rome only because I found that it was impossible to be a Catholic in the Church of my baptism. I tried to be a Catholic in the Church of England because neither my heart nor my mind could find ease in anything but Catholicism, into which I found my way slowly, groping from truth to truth.

The little girl in the brougham bears the same relation to Catholicism that a sprouting acorn bears to an oak tree. The shoots are small and weak, but it is unmistakably the sprouting of the oak, not of the juniper. She has few theological ideas at present, except to be as High Church as parental opposition will allow. The fact that the village church at Brede is very High may have something to do with her ambitions; but there is a genuine attraction in the fuller version of faith she stepped into when she went to school, and she finds it more in keeping than any kind of Protestantism (which she has met in friends and in those little books of evangelical piety beloved of her Presbyterian mother) with what she believed in those far off days of childhood, when she dreamed of heaven and thought (incom-

[8]

prehensibly) that the Pope was the head of the Church.

I wonder what her reactions would have been if I could have appeared to her then as the ghost of her grown-up self and shown her all that the future had in store. A part of the revelation, I know, would have filled her with delight. She would gladly have given up her hopes of the Westfield cottage when I told her that I live in the country northward of Brede, at a farm she mentions in the very first paragraph of her novel, and that the river Tillingham floweth through my very own fields (incidentally giving me a lot of trouble with collapsing banks, foot-bridges and the Catchment Board).

She would also I think be more than satisfied with my literary success. Personally I do not find it dazzling, but she would be enraptured to know that by the time she reached my age she would have had published more than twenty novels, some of which would have attained the (to her) classic status of school books.

She would not have been so pleased to know that before then she would be married (she does not mean to marry, and though she considers herself most romantically in love with one of the boys at the house she is to visit, she would be overwhelmed with shame and horror if she suspected him of the smallest knowledge of it). And she would, I am sure, have protested vehemently if I had told her she would ever join the Church of Rome.

"But I'd never do that," I hear her exclaim in her high, breathless voice. "I could never, *never* do such a thing."

"Why not? You want to be High Church."

"Oh, but that's different. I'd hate to go over to Rome"—her voice drops on a note of contempt. "I'd never change my religion."

"Ah," I'd say, "you haven't read Nietzsche yet."

"Who's Nietzsche?"

"Someone you'll think an oracle in a few years' time."

"But what has he got to do with me changing my religion?"

"He says somewhere—I forget where, but *you*'ll soon know—'A man may not choose to die for his opinions, but he should always be ready to die for the right to hold and change them.'"

"I don't agree with that"—dogmatically. "I think people ought to die for their opinions, but not to change them."

[10]

"Why not? A man who changes his opinions has at least thought about them, which is an improvement on merely holding them. But there's no sense in our arguing like this, for you're not going to change your opinions."

"You said I was."

"Oh, no. What I said was that some day you will join the Church of Rome."

"But how can I do that without changing my opinions—my religion?"

"You'll know when you're as old as I am."

Chapter One

Smith, Kaye and de la Condamine—Crit
Hall and Platnix—the Metamorphoses of
Trimmer—Darsie Forbes and Bran Mhic-
Eagheanh—*Line upon Line*—The School
Atheist—Urbs Beata.

I

WHEN I was a very little girl I used often to wish I
had a grandmother. Grandmothers in the stories I
had read to me were always specially kind and
generous and given to spoiling their grandchildren.
They lived in delightful country houses, with beautiful gardens to play in and ponies to ride. . . . Did
I not know almost by heart *Lottie's Visit to Grand-
mamma*, by a writer called Brenda?

It seemed a great mistake not to have even one of
these excellent relations, whom I knew could be had

[12]

in pairs. But my parents were a middle-aged widow and widower when they met each other, and had both long ceased to have parents of their own. There was no family home on either side to which the children could be taken; even the uncles and aunts were scattered and remote.

As a result I know very little about their families—least of all about my father's. All I know is that he was the son of an Army surgeon and was born in India, a country with which he was connected also on his mother's side. Her brother, Sir John Kaye, was at one time well known as a historian of Indian affairs, and his *History of the Indian Mutiny* was, I believe, a text-book for Army cadets. He also wrote one or two novels, which are completely forgotten.

The Kayes are a Lincolnshire family, springing from the Squire class and closely allied with the Church of England, to which they have given more than one dignitary. When I first saw Bishop Kaye lying on his marble tomb in Lincoln Cathedral, I was immediately struck by his likeness to my father, as I had last seen him, a few hours after his death. The faces were almost identical in their expression of strength and rest and in the features to which

marble and death had given an equal dignity. In life
my father's face was lit up by a pair of blue eyes
that never lost their youthful brightness, shining
with a sort of humorous innocence as they looked
out on a world that always interested and often
delighted him.

I know nothing about the Smith side of his family. My Smith grandfather died young, and I think
it possible that Miss Kaye had not married entirely
to please her relations. Certainly none of her children kept their father's name. Those who did not
marry out of it took hyphens or even dropped it
altogether.

My father took his hyphen last of all, and would
possibly never have done so if he had not married
my mother. Her maiden name was de la Condamine
and she had till the end of her life an unutterable
contempt of Smith. Nothing annoyed her more
than when our Kaye was dropped or taken for a
mere initial. Actually, of course, it is not easy to
live as an undifferentiated Smith, especially in a
town; but I cannot pretend that our hyphen was
not mainly snobbish in origin and intention.

My mother, bless her, was a snob. Or rather, I
should say that there was snob in her, for her char-

acter was a fascinating mixture of opposites. Side by side with the snob went an unpretentious warmth that gave her the love and devotion of a great many humble people. You never knew which side you were going to meet. When I was a girl at school I used to suffer much misery from her refusal to let me go to tea with other girls whom, from devastatingly close inspection of their family trees, she did not consider my social equals. On the other hand I was always allowed to be on terms of absolute equality with the children at the farms where we used to stay or with the children of our servants. There was never any patronizing hint of a difference between us, and the only difference I saw was that of my own obvious inferiority.

My mother's family was altogether another affair racially and religiously from my father's. The de la Condamines left France in the eighteenth century and came to the Channel Islands as Huguenot refugees. They lived first in Jersey and then moved to Guernsey, where one Sunday they all did public penance in the Town Church for having returned to their vomit—in other words, for having attended Mass while on a holiday in France. The Channel Islands were entirely French-speaking in those days, and Robert de la Condamine could speak very little English when he migrated to Edinburgh to start business there as a wine-merchant.

He soon learned enough, however, to marry a Miss MacFarquhar, who saw to it that no French was spoken in her house. He also abandoned for Presbyterianism the very Protestant form of Anglicanism in which he had been brought up. My mother's first husband was the son of a Free Church minister, and to the end of her life she remained strongly Presbyterian in sympathies, though she conformed outwardly to the Church of England after she married my father.

One hears that it is good to be the child of opposites; and if that is so, I am specially fortunate, for I have on one side all that is solid, English and Anglican (though the Smiths have some Scottish blood) and on the other a rather volatile mixture of Scottish and French, Celt and Latin, Presbyterian and Huguenot (with Catholic cravings, if one is to judge by that French holiday). My parents, too, were in themselves as big a contrast as in their families. I remember my father as simple, upright, kind, calm, humorous, thoughtful and slow. My mother, on the other hand was quick, lively, impulsive, variable, contradictory and full of charm till the end of her life. She and my father were admirably suited to each other and most deeply attached. Till death separated them for two sad years they could scarcely ever bear to be apart. They never quarrelled, and if they argued it was in laughter. They always showed each other courtesy and affection.

With a father born of East Anglican stock in India and a mother born of French stock in Edinburgh, it seems almost accidental that I should have been born in Sussex. But my mother had come south on her first marriage, and met my father through the marriage of two of their relations. He had just given up his first practice in the village of Battle, Sussex, and had moved into the neighbouring town of Hastings. Here I was born and here I lived until my marriage. My knowledge of the country outside was due partly to easy access and my love of walking, riding and cycling, partly and principally to my parents' custom of sending my sister and me to stay on farms while they went away together for their holidays.

Compton Mackenzie has stated somewhere that the whole of an author's literary stock-in-trade is laid in before he is twenty-one. After that he can only develop and rearrange impressions already in store. Personally I should reduce this figure by reversing it, and say that an author is conditioned by the time he is twelve. Certainly it was the first twelve years of my life that made me a Sussex novelist.

I still write, I know, from the impressions of those early days—pictures that I see always in a clear sunshine, vivid, alight, and sharp as swords in my memory. In a sense every farm I write of is Platnix Farm, and every human being is one or another of the people that I met there—Daisy and Maudie, the farmer's little girls, their brothers Jesse and George, or the farm men clumping in and out of the kitchen. My very earliest imagination was captured by the country-side that holds it still.

Platnix was not the first farm we stayed at, nor was it the last. But it was the one that most powerfully and permanently captured my heart. Even now when I catch sight of it from the Hastings road, standing with its oast-houses behind three tall poplar trees, I can still revive the ecstasy which I used to feel as I fell asleep on the first night of each return, with one of those tall poplar trees rustling

and shining between me and the daylight sky of
a little girl's bed-time.

2

I have an unusually long memory. Pictures of my
life stretch back into what must have been my very
earliest childhood. They are definitely pictures, that
is to say I can see them clearly, fixed like pictures
on a wall—even if I remember "what happened
next" it is like passing on to another picture. They
are not movies, then, nor are they talkies, but they
are quite distinctly feelies. In most cases I can remember what I felt as keenly as what I saw—marvellous delight and contentment, appalling fears.

One of the earliest is a picture of a tall, thin slice
of a room, softly pervaded with sunlight and the
colour brown. A woman in a dark dress and wearing an apron is standing up beside a table at which I
sit eating rhubarb. A number of wasps are flying
about, but they do not frighten me—in fact there is
no feeling attached to this picture, which is of a
room at Crit Hall, a farm-house near Benenden,
where I stayed one summer when I was two years
old.

The room is not really very high, and the house

[19]

front which I remember as towering up to heaven, is only that of a double-fronted villa, but naturally I see everything in the proportions of those years, and this is emphasized in my next picture, which is charged with acute and terrible feeling up to the very frame of darkness. I am standing in a farm-yard, close to a trug basket filled with crusts of bread, and I am yelling—yelling . . . because I have been given those crusts to feed the chicken, and before I can begin a great big horrible hen has come and helped herself to them. There she is, bobbing her ugly brown neck and crimson comb in and out of my basket, gobbling up everything. I shall have nothing left for the other fowls—I am thwarted, terrified and helpless. She is far too big for me to drive her away, so I just stand there and howl and watch my riches disappear. In the next picture, people are doing their best to comfort me; they have taken me to see some doves—brownish things in a cage, with red berries pushed between the bars for them to eat. I am not really comforted, for my feelings are too painful to be so easily diverted. I still want to feed the fowls, and there are no more crusts to give them.

My last picture is simply of me and a little girl

called Mabel sitting on the ground in front of Crit Hall. The place is huge and clear, but the two human figures are small and dim. I cannot remember Mabel at all; all I know about her is that she is the first of a succession of farm children who from the age of two to twenty were to gladden my heart and kindle my imagination. I have given an account of the Platnix children in a book called *The Children's Summer*, and certainly they outshone the others in a multitude of ways. But there were other children, just as there were other farms.

Platnix came next in time to Crit Hall and was our favourite; in fact with me it soon became an obsession. I was composing verses about Platnix long before I could write; it filled my imagination to such an extent that finally it burst with the conception of the farm-house, as a warrior queen, engaged in battle with the town, and defeating "the ugly houses guarded by city red," to quote from an unwritten work of that period. She smashed their invading forces led by Battle Lodge, our home, and Kesauli, our semi-detached next door; and her praises were sung by the barrel organ that visited us every week, in a tune I called "The Gleam of Platnix Farm," though others called it "The Man Who Broke the Bank at Monte Carlo."

I had at that time, of course, written nothing, though I had made up a few verses and indulged regularly in a ceremony I called "composing." This consisted of marching about with a book and declaiming aloud a story which I professed to read in it. The "heroine" of these stories was a little girl called Trimmer. I have described Trimmer in *The Children's Summer*, and anyone who has read of her there will have recognized her as a fairly obvious example of a wish-fulfilment fantasy. Her adventures were not limited to my hours of "composing"—she lived with me always, though she did not share my life. Clad in dresses made alternatively of solid gold and jewellery or of the massed petals of flowers, Trimmer never had a bath or went to bed. I took care to emancipate her by declaring "Now I'm not Trimmer" whenever these indignities befell me. If I failed to do so it was dreadful and I felt degraded with her. She lived in splendour, power and independence, and represented my escape from the restraints and humiliations of the nursery.

An American reviewer of *The Children's Summer* professed to find in Trimmer a very good reason for my joining the Church of Rome. In Trimmer she saw my first steps in Mariolatry—the setting up of that image which ultimately became the Virgin Mary.

Unfortunately, however, this hypothesis is not borne out by Trimmer's history during the thirty odd years between Platnix Farm and Farm Street.

While we were still at Platnix she acquired a brother Dick. Dick was as naughty as Trimmer was good—("Young Dick he was a heenyus lad" a lay of that period begins)—there was no limit to his daring and wickedness. Obviously he too was a wish-fulfilment, though of another sort. In course of time Trimmer became merely his sister and her name was changed to Rosette. I do not know why the glory departed from her, but it did. He, on the other hand, flourished exceedingly and was renamed Carlo, after the dog belonging to the blind fiddler on the Hastings beach. Then his name was further changed to Adrian, and for the first time a surname was given him—de Cæsar.

Adrian de Cæsar filled for several years an imagination from which Trimmer had vanished completely. His image had swallowed her up as well as Dick, though his position was more subtle than

[23]

either of theirs, for he did not so obviously represent a wish fulfilment. Also he had parents (though these were only seven years older than himself) and a background both in history and geography, for his father was none other than Robert, Duke of Naples, and the family lived on the slopes of Mount Vesuvius. Moreover, unlike Trimmer and Dick, he had a definite story of a tragic, historical kind; in fact, I think he died at the end of it—there is certainly existing in my memory a poem which describes his decease in highly pious and romantic circumstances.

His creator herself nearly made an end at about this time; or perhaps it would be more accurate to say that I cannot understand why I did not die in the course of a holiday at Great Durgates Farm, Wadhurst. We were staying there, as usual, while our parents were abroad, and one afternoon my sister and I discovered that the dullness of the yew trees at the bottom of the garden was relieved by several attractive looking pink berries. These proved pleasant also to the taste and we ate a large number. On returning to the house rather pleased with ourselves it was a shock to be told that they were poisonous.

CHAPTER ONE

Nothing whatever was done about the matter, though I can still see the relative in charge of us hunting through a botany book to discover just how long we had to live. Both my sister and I set up a howl, expecting something dreadful, but when several minutes went by and no symptoms developed, we soon forgot all about it.

As I have said, nothing whatever was done; and nothing whatever happened—which is more than I can explain. Yew-berries are certainly poisonous, and human beings have died of eating them, as well as cattle. My sister and I had eaten quite a number; how was it that we did not feel the slightest gripe or qualm? And how was it that our elders never gave us an emetic or sent for the doctor? When recently I asked one of them why she had done neither of these things, she replied, significantly: "Because you would have been so frightened." No doubt at this time my fears were a terror to all around me, and I had a particular horror of poisonous plants—refusing to let my nurse pick the beautiful *solanum dulcamara*, under the impression that it was deadly nightshade. All the same, when I think now of the fuss I should have made if two children under my care (with parents abroad) had eaten poisonous berries, I am more surprised by the calmness of our elders than by our immunity from what was certainly a deadly poison.

Great Durgates was the last of the Sussex farms we stayed at. We were now of an age to provide at least a semi-rational companionship, and our parents decided that we should all go together to Scotland. This change worked havoc with Adrian de Cæsar, who forthwith became Bonnie Prince Charlie. By the same token, Robert, Duke of Naples, became the Old Pretender; but after a few months I ceased to trouble to adjust my fancy to historical fact. Prince Charlie acquired two brothers and the whole family lived in Strathspey, where we spent our summer holidays for three years in succession.

The Scottish scene had a still more radical effect on my imagination. For the first time the Trimmer —Dick—Carlo—Adrian—Charlie character went off on a separate course from my attempts at fiction. He was no longer the hero of the stories I "composed"; he lived silently and privately in my thoughts, where his descendants are still with me. When after some summers in Scotland we moved our holiday to Devonshire he moved too and changed his surname of Stuart to Drayton. For a time he and his father and brothers maintained their eighteenth-century costumes, though very much as worn by the principal boy in the Hastings Panto-mime; then as I grew older they put on modern dress—indeed their whole tendency has been to ap-proximate themselves more and more closely to life so that if at this stage they were miraculously to materialize, they would—unlike Trimmer—attract no attention from the world around them.

Perhaps their history has been very much that of fiction as a whole, which in the childhood of the world concerned itself entirely with heroes and demi-gods, and then through the adolescence of knighthood and romance has come down to earth, and the common man. No doubt it is only the out-ward presentation that has changed—the inward sig-nificance is the same; and in that sense Trimmer is still with me, though she is no longer "she" or even "he" but "they." In essence she survived my mar-riage and she survived my conversion; all that hap-pened was that when I became a Catholic, "they" became Catholics too, or rather I found that they had always been Catholics—in proof that under-neath it all their wish-fulfilment nature is un-changed.

3

The separation of my two imaginary worlds made a great difference to me as an author. I must call myself an author, though I could scarcely be called a writer, as I now definitely took my "composing" seriously, and planned for the first time my future as the famous novelist Darsie Forbes—to be succeeded as the Celtic fever grew by Bran Mhic-Eagheanh. By the time I was fifteen I had delivered verbally between forty and fifty novels, which I still think must have been full length. I wrote down their titles as I "composed" them, in an exercise book which I have long lost. At the end I was certainly planning them very carefully, writing down the headings of the various chapters and taking almost as much trouble as if they were not to be given to the empty air. I was quite indifferent to an audience and I can't help thinking that this vast literary output (I must in the course of four years have delivered nearly three million words) is one of the purest examples of art for art's sake that any author's history is likely to produce!

The stories all belonged to the Scottish holiday period and were all staged in Scotland, for Scotland had now become for me the passion that Platnix once was, with the added stimulus of a definite sense of place. The place-feeling of Platnix had been implicit rather than realized; but Scotland made me definitely a painter of scenery, a soaker up of atmosphere. I studied maps of the Cairngorms, and I knew the names of mountains as now I know the names of farms. The background to my various tales was always important and carefully chosen. Then as now, I found it impossible to visualize human beings apart from their surroundings; indeed the surroundings often came first, and I would feel an urge to write a tale about the Cromdale hills or the Monadh Liadh mountains before I had populated them, creating my people for the benefit of my place.

When we changed our holiday quarters from Scotland to Devonshire all this came to an end. For one thing, I gave up "composing." Not that I had realized the futility of presenting so much energy, care and invention to the void, but because I thought myself too old to go on with such a childish thing. For some months I had been practising in secret, but grown-ups had listened at the door . . . my privacy was uncertain and I was ashamed. At fifteen I was taking myself very seriously and deliberately decided to lay down my tongue, as it were, and take up my pen.

With my pen—or rather pencil, for ink was too much like school—I returned to Sussex. Scotland had been driven out of my imagination by Devonshire, but Devonshire could not really take a hold. One or two of my early written tales have their scene there, but I had already rediscovered Platnix, and with my bicycle and the long legs of fifteen Platnix was no longer remote and dependent upon the will of my elders. I can still remember the coloured, shining autumn day when walking down Westfield lane, past Cockmartin's Farm—the old Cockmartin, red and sprawling like a squashed pippin, not the new box-like villa that is there now—I suddenly saw it all again with my childhood's eyes. The gleam of Platnix Farm had come back.

4

It is fairly obvious that the imaginative side of me—whether it expressed itself in fantasy or in fiction—found its inspiration only in the holiday part of my life. Neither the characters nor the places had anything to do with my existence for ten months out of the twelve. I never felt inclined to write about a little girl living in a seaside town, or of a hard-working doctor setting out day after day to visit his patients and earn his living. It was not that I considered these things dull or trifling—the small girl in particular was a bottomless well of interest—but they were too close and too accustomed for literary purposes. I wrote about what I had not got and could not see; for at present my imagination was the most fully developed part of me. It was like a young animal, demanding constant exercise, a kitten engaged in a sport that will afterwards become dead earnest.

My religion, on the other hand, belonged to every day—to Hastings and the ten non-holiday months. It was something quite apart from my two imaginary worlds—the world of Trimmer and her descendants and the world of my forty-odd novels. It was all mixed up with common things like eating and drinking (grace before meals), getting up and going to bed (when I said my prayers), being naughty (when I was told I displeased God) and being good (when I was said to please Him).

I certainly never felt inclined to write about it; but, in a different way, I was just as deeply preoccu-

pied with it as with the things I wrote about. In this
I believe I was like rather than unlike most other
children. Most children if given the smallest religious idea will grasp hold of it and show a curiosity
that is at least equal to, if not greater than, that early
pre-occupation with sex we hear so much about.
And even without a single religious idea being given
it the normal child will probably of itself sooner or
later ask the first two questions of the Catholic
Penny Catechism—"Who made me?" and
"Why?" . . .

My elders were able to give me the answer to
the first question, though they were not so clear
about the second, in spite of the fact that my
mother must have learned in the Shorter Catechism
of her Presbyterian days an answer which is doctrinally the same as that of the more long-winded
Penny Catechism—"the chief end of man is to
glorify God and enjoy Him for ever." Why is it,
by the way, that the Catechism of the Church of
England ignores both these primitive and instinctive questions, substituting for the first the public
school formula of What is your name?

The theology of those early days was certainly
vague; nevertheless I came out of them with cer-

tain very clear conceptions—God—Christ—Heaven —Redemption—Judgment—Hell. My knowledge was drawn mainly from those two Victorian classics—*Line upon Line* and *The Peep of Day*. It is the fashion now to deride them, and I have known moderns who blame them for the whole of their hell-fire complex; but they had no effect of that kind on me. On the contrary, they fed my growing interest in the supernatural, and gave me a working knowledge of both the Old and the New Testaments before I was able to read. Apart from this, I found them so interesting as mere story-telling that I went on reading them for my own pleasure long after my elders had given them up as books of instruction. As for the hell fire, it did not worry me at all. I was an exceedingly nervous child, afraid of high buildings, big trees, Christmas crackers, striking clocks, ghosts, bath-chair attendants, dogs, beggars and having my hair washed, but I was not afraid of hell. Even the hell fire sermons we heard in Scotland, which were often replete with lurid details, could move me to nothing stronger than interest or occasionally (if the minister stamped very hard) to laughter. I suppose I was just not hell conscious.

This does not mean that I did not believe in hell—simply that I was not afraid of going there. It had never in my nursery days been held over me as a threat, and I remember how, later on, my sister and I mocked and jeered when an exasperated governess tried to frighten us with Dr. Watts's poems. I regarded hell as the exclusive abode of excitingly wicked people, with whom a little girl like me could not except to be included. Heaven, on the other hand, both my temperament and my teaching encouraged me to hope for, and I parted willingly with my belief in fairies on being told that the angels did not have to go too. God was a rather distant Father—a little farther off than heaven, I think; and the foreground was filled with the friendly figure of His Son. As a very small child I had an almost romantic devotion to Our Lord, and always set aside the letter J among my letter-biscuits, consuming it with a special veneration, until someone unkindly told me that it also stood for Judas.

Another early belief of mine is more difficult to account for. I believed that the Pope was Head of the Church. How I acquired this doctrine it would be hard to say, for I had it before we began

CHAPTER ONE

our sequence of French nursery-governesses; but
though I cannot remember its origin I know that
when my elders at last discovered it in the course of
a history lesson, I did not give it up without argument.

I am writing now of a very little girl, not more
than seven or eight years old. In those days religion was a real thing, as Platnix was a real thing,
and it too had a gleam. . . . I sometimes wonder
what would have happened if I had been a Catholic
child and this deep absorption and delight had been
given their normal outlet in a Sacramental life.
Perhaps I am inclined to exaggerate the difference
it would have made, for no doubt I am more to
blame than my elders for all I lost as I grew up.
My elders did their duty in pointing out to me that
my aspirations after God and heaven were vain
if I was not also "a good little girl." It was not
their fault that such admonitions necessarily
plunged me into a sea of resentful struggle, in
which after a time it scarcely seemed worth while
to keep afloat.

I suppose that most religiously brought up children who come to lose their native pleasure in religion, do so because they are choked off it by too

much church-going or too heavily pious exercises. My superiors did not make that mistake with me— I did not till I was eleven or twelve go to church regularly every Sunday, and I had lost my first fine rapture long before then. No, the trouble was that they used religion for their own ends, as a means to securing my good behaviour. They emphasized the bread side of piety and decried the circuses. They could not understand how while I loved the hymn that begins

> Around the throne of God a band
> Of glorious angels ever stand

I hated that which admonishes "little children weak" to "stay the angry blow" and "check the hasty word."

> Give gentle answers back again
> And fight a battle for our Lord.

I am not suggesting that angry blows and hasty words become those who seek the company of angels, but I still think that too much stress can be laid on mere good conduct, and the temptation to use other people's religion as leverage to get what we want out of them is only too insidious for grown-up people in charge of naughty children.

CHAPTER ONE

Be that as it may, my religion collapsed under the weight of morality laid upon it, and by the time I went to school, which I did at the age of nine, it had entirely lost its place in my imagination. Not that I doubted its reality or neglected to say my prayers—but it was no longer "the apple tree, the singing and the gold." It was Being Good, Keeping my Temper, Doing my Homework, Never Missing my Practising—just as bad in a different way as if it had been exclusively Going to Church. It had become a part of my bondage as a little girl; I never spoke of it and I thought of it as little as possible. Lost in a subjective world of frustration, I fought as one beating the air.

Yet some of the old magic must have lingered, for one of the most painful memories of my school-days is the week I spent as an atheist.

I use the word advisedly, for it was at the bottom of all my trouble. I met it for the first time in the pages of *We Two* a novel by Edna Lyall. Careful Catholic parents who nurture their children apart from all suggestions of unorthodox propaganda may well lay this to heart. My seducer was no crafty rationalist, no iconoclastic follower of Darwin or Huxley or Hackel, but a blameless lady writing blameless books for girls.

I wonder if Edna Lyall is still read. I think she deserves to be, for though her men are invariably women dressed in men's clothes, and her whole view of life is over-sublimated, she tells a good story and sets it against a richly filled-in background that is often seen from an original point of view. She was a great champion of unpopular causes and *We Two* is a vindication of Charles Bradlaugh—not of his beliefs, for she was an earnest churchwoman, but of his sincerity. I had not got far into it before I came across the disruptive word.

"What's an atheist?" I asked.

"Somebody who believes there is no God."

"Oh . . ."

I was shocked into silence. I had not known that anybody lived who could believe such a thing, that such an attitude of mind was possible. It was the same as if I had been told that there were people who doubted the existence of tables and chairs. The self-evident was rejected, and no recourse to reason or to authority could restore it; for the mere fact that it was possible to doubt these things

[38]

was enough to shatter the whole of my invisible world. If people, grown-up people, learned people like the man in this book, believed there was no God, they were just as likely to be right as the people who did believe in them. Perhaps it was true that there was no God. In that case, who had made me! Perhaps nobody. And where would I go when I died? Perhaps nowhere.

The doubt ate up my poor little mind as a lion might eat up a sparrow and as a sparrow I was helpless. I did not try to defend myself, I did not reason or argue, and I did not cry for help to my elders. It was all too horrible, and I shut the horror up in my soul. I simply did not dare tell anyone that I had the temerity—for sometimes it seemed temerity rather than helplessness—to doubt what everyone around me believed. I walked in agony alone.

There is in my mind a picture of myself in those days. I am drilling in the school gymnasium, but it is only the usual exercise between classes and I do not wear a gym dress. I wear instead a garment of humiliation—no less than the first dress which on my growing out of it has not been made over to my sister. Instead, her dress and mine have by some foul alchemy of the sewing-machine been transmuted into one—I can see its dull brown colour and puffed sleeves, and the braid at the waist designed to conceal the unholy alliance of her skirt and my bodice. My taste in dress was entirely negative; I had a horror of being made to wear what I did not like, and I was wearing it today. And on top of it all I was an atheist. Marching down the centre of the room in a long line of girls to the strains of Sousa's "Stars and Stripes" on the gymnasium piano, I shuddered at the thought of the spiritual gulf that separated me from those on whose heels I was treading. I did not suppose that any other little girl had ever been an atheist and the thought of my singularity brought me no comfort, only an increase of gloom. I felt a pariah and an outcast.

Then suddenly it all cleared up. The suggestion was removed, not by a counter-suggestion but by an elementary reasoning process. The month was January, and the feast of the Conversion of St. Paul was celebrated by a hymn at our school prayers. It occurred to me that if there was no God, St. Paul could not have been converted. He could not have seen a vision if there had been no one to see, or heard a voice if there had been none to hear, nor would he have gone round the world on those tiresome missionary journeys that had such a disastrous effect on my marks in the Religious Knowledge lesson if he had not been quite sure that what he preached was true. Of course he was sure, because, unlike me or the atheist in the book, he had definite first-hand information. Hooray! I believed it all again. "Our soul hath been delivered even as a sparrow . . ."

5

One would think, perhaps, that this deliverance would have restored me to some of my lost delight in religion; but it did nothing of the kind. The weight of morality remained exactly as before. After all, if my doubts had done nothing to lighten this burden—for they could make no practical difference while my elders had charge of my life—it was unlikely that their removal would make it any easier to bear. I still chafed under the Law, even though I now knew how utterly void and dreadful a Lawless world could be. I disliked going to church, which was now regarded as part of my duty, and when my Confirmation was spoken of

I drew back, strangely shocked and raw, into a shell of silent opposition.

This attitude lasted till the summer of my sixteenth year, which was spent at East Week, a farm near Throwleigh in Devon. It was our first English holiday after the Scottish interlude, and the first time for many years that I had gone to church in the country. Throwleigh Church was small, simple and engagingly countrified—something quite different from the big, dark church at home; and it provided quite a different form of service. The difference did not lie only in simplicity, but in the fact that Throwleigh Church was distinctly High. On at least one occasion a celebration of Holy Communion was substituted for the accustomed Morning Prayer. Though I was so soon to be Confirmed, this was the first time that I had been present at Holy Communion. I knew very little about it, though I had, of course, many times heard the Table Prayers—that is the first part of the Anglican Communion Service, which is often read as a part of morning worship on Sunday. As a child I had often felt perplexed when, just as things were beginning to get interesting, the organ had started to play and the congregation to march out. I should certainly have been annoyed if I had not been allowed to march with them, but I could not help wondering what happened after we had gone.

To-day I was to know, for the organ did not play for exit, and a whispered conversation took place among our elders as to what was to be done with my sister and me. It was decided that my sister, aged thirteen, should be taken out, but that I, fifteen and soon to be Confirmed, might very well stay. So I stayed, and was given back something which I had lost. That service gave me back my perception of what has been called the numinous side of religion—the shining cloud, the Shekinah, without which the Temple is merely a heap of stones—the gleam.

This restoration did not come through any liturgical beauties, for everything was of the plainest, humblest kind (I think I was most impressed by the three women communicants, one of whom was the farmer's wife at East Week). It was rather that here for the first time I saw the Church. Hitherto —ever since the instinctive religion of childhood had passed—religion had been a strictly personal affair, governed by rules of conduct. Now for the first time I saw myself as one of a company, approaching God, not merely to win His favour by our good behaviour, but to do Him honour and to give Him praise and to receive in exchange those gifts which I had vaguely sensed as a child but had never apprehended until now.

It is, of course, difficult to say exactly how much of all this I realized on this one occasion, but certainly at about this time I came to know something of the union between God and man in His Sacraments. I longed for the fellowship of the altar, and thenceforward instead of dreading my Confirmation I passed my time in eager expectation of the day.

It came three months later, and I shall always remember the joy of seeing my whole life stretch before me in the light of that experience. Religion had recovered its lost "gleam," and with it the whole of life had taken colour and romance. Also it was at about this time that I definitely started writing, as distinct from "composing" and that I came back, as it were, into Sussex, recapturing the "gleam of Platnix Farm." My life was trebly shining and I remember my sixteenth and seventeenth years as a period of especial happiness.

CHAPTER ONE

Good conduct had been lifted out of dullness on romantic wings and a certain amount of religious instruction both at church and at school had brought a little of my mind and reason into the business. The country was no longer remote—I found myself in it every week, on foot, on horseback or on my bicycle—and it was now linked up with religion by my memories of Throwleigh Church and by the fact that Brede Church was just as High as Throwleigh. As for my novels—no longer subjective promises to the air but objective performances on paper—they brought the country and religion together in a clandestine delight. I wrote them illicitly when I should have been doing my homework, and I gave up writing them as an act of self-denial during Lent.

Chapter Two

My fifty-sixth novel—Rouge and forget-me-nots—Prayer from Limbo—An experiment with time—The author of *The Tramping Methodist*—Just what a novelist would do.

I

MY OUTPUT of fiction is rather like an iceberg; by far the greater part of it is out of sight. The visible part consists of twenty-two published novels, but invisible under the water lies the mass of my forty-two "composed" novels, and the thirteen novels I wrote during my last two years at school. The latter did not in any way approach the length of the former—in fact, strictly speaking, they were not novels at all, as the longest does not run to more than twenty thousand words, and the short-

[46]

est works out at scarcely more than half that. Nevertheless, as I wrote at least six a year, this was no mean effort for a schoolgirl who has to fit her writing into her ordinary school routine, including three hours' daily music practice. In fact, looking back on it now from my present rate of achievement, I don't know how I did it.

But I did it, because I have all the volumes in proof—dozens of green exercise books—"fifty pages for one penny"—darkened with pencil and smeary with india-rubber. I wrote entirely for my own private pleasure without a thought of publication, though I was still determined to be a famous author one day. I read some of the tales to my sister, and of one I made a fair copy, bound it and presented it to my mother; but in each case this happened some time after the work was finished. When it was new and fresh in my consciousness I could not bear any eye to see it but my own.

Of these thirteen novelettes four are staged in Devonshire, and the rest belong to Sussex. All except two are historical. I was a devourer of historical novels, especially those written by Edna Lyall, who had almost as devastating an effect on my literary style at this period as she had once had

on my religious beliefs. All without any exception
are tales of gloom and woe. One or two are allowed
a happy ending, but they all abound in death
scenes, partings, swoonings, fightings, frustrations,
and undying regrets. In this they were not unlike
the Scottish stories. My muse was always melancholy, and at this age I had no interest in humour
at all—regarding it as something occasionally inevitable in private life, but always degraded and
having no place in superior fiction.

These schoolgirl stories are obvious predecessors
of my first two published novels—*The Tramping
Methodist* and *Starbrace*. Not only are these both
historical, but one of them deals with a subject
that had already filled half a dozen of the penny
exercise books. I had written two highwayman tales
called respectively *Sion Hall* and *Merriment Farm*,
and in *Starbrace* I deliberately used again scenes
and characters that seemed as good to me at twenty-
one as they had seemed at sixteen.

Re-reading those early works to-day, I am struck
by their sentimentality, their unreality, their third-
hand impression of everything except the country
outside Hastings. Of character-drawing there is
hardly a vestige—the characters, men and women

[48]

CHAPTER TWO

alike, are all dressed-up schoolgirls, except perhaps
the highwaymen, who, being drawn entirely from
my imagination without any help from Edna Lyall,
come a little closer to life as it may have been.
The stories themselves are unlikely and badly con-
structed, though here some of the faults may be
due to lack of revision. Occasionally there is a
well-imagined if badly executed scene or situation,
and often a real feeling for beauty and history in
the Sussex country-side. But certainly my first two
published novels, crude as they are, are master-
pieces in comparison. One might say that the chief
promise of those schoolgirl tales lies in the fact
that they were written—that I should have had the
perseverance and devotion to cover all those endless sheets of paper without any encouragement
beyond that given me by my own naïve delight in
my performance.

I do not know when I first came to think of publication. I certainly had no idea of it when I started
to write my first published novel, *The Tramping
Methodist*. I can remember exactly how that novel
began—there is the clearest picture of it in my
mind.

I am lying in bed—in a high, shapeless feather

bed—in a room in a farm-house known as Botvyle.
The window looks into a farmyard, and at right-
angles to it "the old part of the house" juts out.
The blind is drawn, but through its papery pale-
ness I can see the outline of the old black and white
gable, and on the peak of the gable sits the shadow
of a robin. At that moment a number of vague
things rush together in my mind—they have been
lying scattered about it for some time, but now
they suddenly cohere into a purpose. I shall write
a novel called *The Romance of a Methodist*, all
about the wanderings of a Methodist preacher
through the country I love best—Brede, Ewhurst,
Ticehurst and the Rother Valley, and perhaps away
across the Kent Ditch to Rolvenden and Benenden
and Tenterden. . . . It shall be a real, full-length
novel, filling at least ten of the penny exercise
books, and when it is finished I shall make a fair
copy of it, with red-ink margins, as I made of *Iden*,
and give it to my mother. I shall illustrate it, too,
with photographs, and there shall be a robin in it.

I cannot remember exactly how or when this
purpose changed to the more ambitious one of
writing the book for publication. But change it did,
as well as the title, at some time and for some rea-

son in the course of the following year. I told nobody of my plan either before or after it changed. Everyone was used to seeing me writing, and everyone knew better than to ask me what I was writing about.

2

It took me just under a year to write *The Tramping Methodist* which seems slow compared with my earlier achievements, especially as now I had left school and there was no competition from homework. I had, however, written the book exactly twice, making a fair copy which was almost another story. I was also distracted in a certain measure by the business of growing up. That year saw me "come out" at the local Hunt Ball. I should properly have done this a year earlier, when I first left school, but I looked and was so ludicrously young for my age that my mother decided to keep me back. It was almost a year later that I stood hopefully in the Drill Hall at Battle, expecting the very best of life and mankind, and wearing a cream lace dress, forget-me-nots and goloshes. The last were an oversight and belonged to the rigours of a two hours' cab drive in January. The lace dress was, I think, quite pretty in itself, though it did not suit me, and I was far too pale to wear forget-me-nots.

I enjoyed the dance, but I did not care for those other aspects of social life to which it was the portal. I disliked the Edwardian routine—paying calls and going to "At Homes" and card parties. They interfered with my writing and with my wanderings in the country, and they provided nothing in the way of personal triumph to woo me from those austerer pleasures. I was not the sort of girl likely to be a social success at that period, or (let us be honest) at any other. I disliked talking except about things that interested me, I was not pretty and I was not well dressed—even by Edwardian provincial standards. I bought my hats inconceivably at the ironmonger's and had my suits made by a tailor whose dislike of new fashions amounted almost to a phobia.

Make-up was of course forbidden to the respectable girlhood of those days, but on this account I was scarcely orthodox, for though I never wore powder I occasionally wore rouge, encouraged by my mother herself. She did not like to see me looking pale, and with her entire approval I daubed each cheek from a little box before going out to dances. We both imagined the crime to be undetectable, but when I remember that in those days rouge was provided in only one shade of vivid carmine, and that I wore no powder to soften the edges, I can only think that the result had something to do with the empty spaces on my programme.

It was, perhaps, as well that I had not the usual ambitions of my age and that my mind was full of plans with which my personal appearance had very little to do. I had finished a book, and my chief if not my only care was to find a publisher for it. I was pleased with the work on the whole, but I felt diffident about certain parts and longed for expert advice. It did not even occur to me to assault some well-known author with my manuscript; I took instead what still seems to me the better course of sending it to the Reading Branch of the Society of Authors. This cost me a guinea, and a guinea is a difficult sum to come by when one's allowance is only a shilling a week; but I managed it with the help of Christmas and a saving disposition, and the Society of Authors duly received a Postal Order

and the manuscript of *The Tramping Methodist*—
a novel by E. S. Ticehurst.

This, the last of my pen-names, was assumed, not
so much out of shyness or diffidence as out of the
desire to be taken for a man. At that time I would
have given all I possessed to be a man, and the next
best thing was to be taken for one in print. This
also accounts for the many violent episodes in
the story. I hoped that these would incline its readers to think that E. S. stood for Edward Samuel
rather than Emily Sheila; though I cannot think
why I did not take a man's name outright—I certainly had not the scruples of Currer Bell.

However, E. S. Ticehurst had only a brief
career. I abandoned him on the advice of the Society's reader, whose Report had in my eyes the infallibility of a Papal decree. He certainly gave me
far more than a guinea's worth of good counsel;
his detailed criticism enabled me to remove the
more glaring of the book's crudenesses and to put
the whole thing into better shape. I had asked him
whether he thought it good enough to send to a
publisher and he replied that he did, which encouraged me to such a pitch that I cast aside the
cloak of secrecy which had wrapped me and my

doings until then and displayed myself to my family as a real, professional author. I had written a book which the Society of Authors said was good enough to send to a publisher, and I was going to send it.

Actually I sent it to an agent. I am not quite clear why I did this, and in those days the Society of Authors was opposed to Literary Agents for beginners. Nevertheless, when I insisted, they recommended the Literary Agency of London, and the Agency expressed its willingness to read my manuscript "provided it was typewritten."

Here arose a new and entirely unforeseen obstacle. The manuscript was beautifully written, with all the margins ruled in red ink; but apparently that was not enough, and inquiry showed that to have it typewritten would cost the quite impossible sum of three pounds, twelve and six. What was to be done? I consulted my parents, who came to the rescue, not by giving me the money but by lending it.

Repayment was no empty form, though in the end they had to remit ten shillings of the loan, as I never succeeded in mustering more than three pounds, two and sixpence. Ten shillings of this

I earned by cleaning the stairs every day for a month, and two pounds twelve and six by going back for a term to my old school as a sort of auxiliary teacher. The last experience I found quite hateful. Neither a mistress nor a girl, I was equally beset by both. Most of the girls had actually been at school with me, and regarded my reappearance as a sort of joke, while the mistresses were rightly annoyed by the uproar that came from any classroom I was functioning in. Nothing could have brought me more relief than the inevitable sack.

3

Meanwhile *The Tramping Methodist* had done little to reward me for these efforts. I had had some encouraging praise from the Literary Agency of London when it read the manuscript, but the high hopes raised by this soon died when the book was rejected by Messrs. Hodder & Stoughton, the first publishers to whom it was sent.

After that came some blank months. The Agency had announced that it would not report any further rejections, but would write only if and when the book was accepted. Time passed in silence. I knew that my Methodist was tramping from door to door in Fleet Street and Paternoster Row (where the publishers still lived in those days), but I had no means of following his progress or of assisting it—save by prayer.

In prayer I indulged freely. The religion of that time, as I remember it, was little more than prayer for the success of *The Tramping Methodist*. For I have to confess that once again the supernatural had failed me, and once again I have to apportion the blame between myself and external thwartings. These lay this time in the sphere of doctrine rather than in the sphere of conduct. I had wanted to be High Church. Both the circumstances of my revived interest in religion and the nurture that religion had been given at school combined to encourage this desire. I will not pretend that it was founded on conviction, nor will I acknowledge that it was based entirely on emotion. It had about it a strong instinctive urge, something like an animal's sense of direction. A cat will find his way home over an unknown road many miles long, guided entirely by his sense of direction, and I once had a dog whom it was impossible to take for a walk unless his nose was never allowed to be turned in the direction of home. Once he faced a certain point in the compass, off he went; and so did I—knowing probably no more intelligently and no less instinctively than he did that it was the way home. And, like him, I was thwarted by human beings with the very best intentions. I wanted to be High Church, but I was not allowed. The local High Church was disapproved of, and I was forbidden to go there, as well as to join any High Church guild or societies, or even to make the Sign of the Cross. My parents were not tyrannical and my home was a very happy one, but they were of their generation in ordering their children's lives.

My surrender was no doubt due to the repercussions of that earlier battle which I had lost. I was still so steeped in the idea that religion consists of "being good," that I could not in this new crisis shake myself free of infantile standards or believe that I had the right to make my own soul. My attitude seems ridiculous to me now, and I have no doubt but that if I had shown tact and sense I could have carried my point with two reasonable people, both of whom loved me sincerely. But tact and sense are adult qualities, and it must be remembered that though in actual age I was a young woman, in temperament I was still a child, and a child inhibited by false religious stresses which had interfered with my normal spiritual growth. I gave up my High Church ambitions, for unfulfilled they tormented me; and in giving them up I gave up much of religion itself. My religious life—over-sublimated, under-instructed and entirely subjective— could not stand up of itself, and soon sank into that borderland between religion and superstition where prayer is only the voice of a greedy child crying Gimme . . . Gimme . . . I want . . . I want . . . I want *The Tramping Methodist* to be published. Please God, make somebody publish *The Tramping Methodist*.

In due course of time Messrs. George Bell & Sons were made to publish *The Tramping Methodist*. Seemingly endless years had gone by, but it was actually no more than seven months after the manuscript had been first sent out that I came down to breakfast and saw lying by my place the Agency's pale blue envelope with its corner design of dark blue scroll work. As they had told me they would not write to record rejections, only when the novel was accepted, I felt sure that this must mean an acceptance. "Oh," said I to myself, "it's just as I dreamt it."

For that night I had dreamed of going down to breakfast, seeing a letter from the Agency beside my plate, and guessing that it meant the acceptance of my manuscript. Then I had gone down to breakfast and found it all exactly as I had dreamed. Then I had woken up.

For the second going down to breakfast had been still in my dream—in the second dream I had dreamed of myself remembering the first one. Now I was doing it all for the third time. Was I going to wake up a third time and find it all a dream? The fear that I might do this was actually strong enough to spoil the first few moments of my rapture, but as time passed and I did not awake I came to the conclusion that the third experience was final and genuine. *The Tramping Methodist* was accepted, and incidentally my dream consciousness had made a very neat experiment with time.

Till then, though I was always a dreamer, I had never "dreamed true"; since then I have done so repeatedly, though subsequent dreams have been mostly of unimportant events, presented in the normal manner of dreamland, with masses of irrelevant and grotesque detail. In the case of the first dream there was nothing redundant or impossible—I dreamed the bare facts exactly as they happened. The chance that what I dreamed was mere coincidence is reduced not only by this literalness but by the fact that the odds against the agents writing as they did on this especial day must have been considerable; for the book had been only seven months on the road, and as everyone knows a first novel may wander round for years.

I was amazed, but the amazement of the dream was soon swallowed up by the amazement of the waking reality. My book was accepted, and would be printed. It would also be paid for, though the financial side of the business was not the most impressive, either in fact or in my imagination. I was to be given twenty pounds in consideration of the first thousand copies sold, and thereafter a shilling each copy—a very good royalty for a beginner, if I had ever received it, which I never did, as *The Tramping Methodist* sold only eight hundred and fifty copies.

The publisher wanted to see me, and an appointment was duly made; but my pleasure and excitement were a little dashed when I found that my parents absolutely refused to let me go to his office unchaperoned. Such a course would in their opinion have forfeited my right to all human respect, including the publisher's. "He'd think nothing of you if he saw you were allowed to do such a thing." . . . So my father escorted me to my interview with the head of the firm, who I'm sure would have been highly surprised had he known of the parental reaction to his suggestion.

My memory has a clear picture of the scene—the large, pleasantly furnished room that surprised me so much (I don't know what I had expected), the publisher at his desk, grave and elderly and eminently to be trusted alone with any young woman, my father in his corner, beaming solemnly and never speaking unless spoken to (though I did not altogether approve of his escort I certainly could not accuse him of stealing my big scene), while I sat close to the desk, quivering with excitement and exhaustion (I was virtually fasting, having eaten almost nothing for two days). I had chosen my costume with especial care—a dark green cloth skirt hitched to a white nainsook blouse by an enormous safety-pin, which was hidden by a petersham belt. On my head I wore a brown straw

CHAPTER TWO

hat, on my feet black shoes and black cotton stock-
ings. Mercifully, I never put on rouge in daylight,
so it was left to my emotions to colour my face,
which they did more naturally, though not more
becomingly, as they also induced an abundant per-
spiration. To the publisher, to his reader, who also
interviewed me, and to my agent, I must have appeared the rawest, greenest author of all their experience. They were, however, exceedingly kind
and encouraging, and I left them almost convinced
that a brilliant career lay ahead of me.

And did I in my hour of triumph thank the
heaven which had answered my prayer? I suppose
I did, but I do not remember it, and I do not think
the thanksgiving was half as fervent as the prayer.
Besides, I still had a lot to pray for, as my novel
was not yet published, and all my religious emotions were concentrated on that. The lost gleam
of religion now rested upon authorship. Indeed authorship was blazing like the sun and I saw nothing
save in its light.

4

The next few months were hectic with antici-
pation. I corrected my first set of proofs in the

[63]

spirit of one performing a solemn religious rite—
or rather, perhaps, a dangerous surgical operation,
for I was in terror of making a mistake and hesi-
tated between one word and another as if my
Methodist's life depended on it. Yet in spite of all
my care a cancel leaf had to be inserted at the last
moment after the book was printed. In straining
after commas I had let slip the moon, which I
had allowed to rise twice on the same evening,
once as a "full, round disc" and then a few hours'
later as "a thin, shining crescent." I doubt if many
publishers to-day would spend so much trouble
and money on a mere astronomical nicety.

Perhaps the reason was that Messrs. George Bell
had not been hitherto publishers of fiction, con-
fining themselves rather to educational and religious books. They were making a new departure
with my novel, and they gave me, I think, an exceedingly good start. The book was well printed,
well bound and well advertised; it was also exceedingly well reviewed. The publishers in their
advertisements had made wise publicity of my
youth, and the critics were therefore more ready
to forgive me a plot that was a tangle of impossi-
bilities and a view of life that was obviously sec-

ond-hand and derived from other books. A few
of them pointed out that it was clear I knew
nothing of Methodism, and had merely used my
hero's denomination as an excuse for his wanderings through a beloved country-side. In fact, most
of them, I think, realized that my protagonist was
really the country of the Rother Valley and my
plot a map of the Kent and Sussex borders. I was
lucky to meet so much tolerance and understanding
on my first appearance; for, sensitive as I had always been about my writing, I should have suffered badly from a harsh reception—and critics
could be really harsh in those days of unsigned reviews.

A further advantage of my good press was that
it enabled me to hold my head up in my native
town, where the publication of *The Tramping
Methodist* had been a nine days' wonder. No one,
except a few close friends sworn to secrecy, had
heard anything about it beforehand, and its sudden appearance at the local libraries struck with
amazement those excellent ladies and gentlemen
who knew me only as an awkward and silent girl
with bookish tendencies and extraordinary clothes.

They were still more amazed when they read

the novel. Among the first novels of to-day *The Tramping Methodist* would appear a very harmless work, its violence the mere fizzing of soda-water; but in 1908 things were different. Then girls were supposed to read—and presumably, if they ever wrote, to write—"books for girls." The masculinity of *The Tramping Methodist*—either aped or the genuine expression of the adolescent boy-girl—to say nothing of the nature of the story, which contained a murder trial and lurid prison scenes, would be a severe shock to anyone expecting Pixie O'Shaughnessy. Some local readers, including the editor of the Hastings newspaper, were charmingly appreciative, and some no doubt were excellently amused; but as far as certain others were concerned, I might just as well have called on my publisher without a chaperon.

Those were the days of the Suffragist movement—if such a slow word can be used to describe so many swift occasions—and women everywhere were making themselves unpopular by the discovery that certain deeds may arouse at least the compliment of an opposition from those on whom one's most desperate words have fallen as the gentle rain. At that time I took no interest whatsoever in any politics later than the French Revolution, but it was taken for granted by the good ladies of Hastings and St. Leonards that being a novelist I must also be a Suffragette. Novelists were well known to be emancipated, and Suffragettes were even more notoriously emancipated, so it followed in logic that I being avowedly guilty on one count must also be guilty on the other.

Rumour knocked me down and blacked my eyes. I did not mind, for I was not opposed to Women's Suffrage—just not interested (I should think better of myself now if then I had at least done a little to help win that nothing which should have been so much). I did not really mind—though my family did—when I was accused of burning down Levetleigh, the Borough Member's house, which stood opposite ours.

It was destroyed one night, almost certainly by Suffragists, and I remember the bitter disappointment with which, on waking the next morning, I realized what a spectacle I had missed. I had never seen a fire, and this by all accounts had been a specially splendid and satisfactory one. I felt a little ashamed of having slept through it. Therefore great was my surprise when I heard that I myself had done the deed. The evidence was clear—I had sat at the window, mocking the efforts of the fire-brigade and shouting "Votes for Women!" The firemen themselves had seen me and had told the police.

For a time things looked unpleasant, and might really have been so if my father had not succeeded in establishing my innocence, at least in official quarters. Nearer to indignation than I have ever seen him in my life, he visited the police-station, he visited the headquarters of the fire-brigade, he visited his club, where the scandal died last of all—if indeed it can be said to have died, for I believe that there are still people who think that I burned down Levetleigh. It is just the sort of thing a novelist would do.

Chapter Three

The author of *Starbrace*—The lights of London—A room of one's own—The will to disbelieve—Swedenborg and *Spell Land*—Emancipation—Downwards to the street.

I

BEFORE *The Tramping Methodist* was even accepted I had started another book, so that six months after my first novel was published the second was ready to appear. I have already said that these two novels are really the last of my schoolgirl outpourings. But for their length and superior merit due to the fact that they had been carefully revised there is very little difference between them and the contents of the penny exercise books. I had made perhaps more of an attempt at character-drawing in the second than in the first, and shown a more adult sense of tragedy, but the theme is the old one of highwaymen and their desperate deeds that delighted my girlhood—though the adventures of Michael Daunt in *Starbrace* are more realistically sordid and sinister than those of his namesake in *Merriment Farm* or of his literary ancestor Sir Jimmy Raikes (Jimmy-go-to-the-Devil to his friends) in *Sion Hall*.

Both *Starbrace* and *The Tramping Methodist* have this in common—the male characters are better realized and less wooden than the female. I had no brothers and practically no male acquaintance, but from the days of Adrian de Cæsar men rather than women had held my imagination, and it was from my imagination that I wrote entirely. My own observation provided nothing but the country-side, and even that appeared less as I saw it with my grown-up eyes than as I had first seen it as a child at Crit Hall and Platnix.

Starbrace had just as good a press as *The Tramping Methodist*, and was just as bad for my local reputation. I can now realize a little of what my parents must have had to go through at this time. They themselves no doubt had expected me to write something very different and were as deeply surprised at my rogues and vagabonds as any old lady in the town. But they stood by me loyally in public and offered very few criticisms in private; though I have in my mind a sharply etched picture of my mother poised on the top bar of a stile and exclaiming passionately without context: "Sheila, you're *not* to say, 'I like 'em full-breasted.'"

They both took my literary career very seriously; so seriously, in fact, that they were willing in its interests to modify their attitude of social correctness. This was mainly my mother's, as her family pride required that I should be more closely guarded than any other young maiden in Hastings or St. Leonards. Long after my school friends were going about alone, I was always accompanied by a French maid, and it was not till I was nearly twenty-one that I was allowed to cross London without an escort. Her reactions to publishers have already been described, and it is therefore rather surprising that less than a year after that episode I should find myself staying alone at a club in Piccadilly.

I owe this emancipation chiefly to my literary agent. He had told me bluntly that it was a pity I led such a sheltered life. I ought to know more of the world—it would help me; in fact, it was essential to me, as a novelist. The public did not really care for historical novels, hence the small sales of my two (*Starbrace* had sold even less than *The Tramping Methodist*). What the public wanted in the year 1909 was drawing-room comedies, but drawing-room comedies are not apparently written in drawing-rooms. If I would really succeed I must come out of the drawing-room into a less restricted atmosphere.

Deeply impressed, I repeated all this to my father and mother, who accepted it as an authoritative opinion on an important question. We talked the matter over and decided that I had better join a club and stay there a fortnight—at my parents' expense. So off I went to London and stayed a fortnight at a ladies' club. But it did not inspire me to write a drawing-room comedy.

It did not, in fact, make any appreciable difference to my literary style or to my knowledge of modern life. I spent that fortnight almost entirely alone, either sitting in the club reading magazines or walking about the streets of an unknown city. Sometimes I went for a 'bus ride, but as I had been in town a considerable time before I learned to read the destinations of 'buses, to board one was rather too much of a venture for real enjoyment. Often I felt desperately lonely and longed to go home. My chief pleasures were eating chocolate éclairs at Lyons' or Liptons' and visiting a Hastings family who had a house in town. But for them I scarcely know what I should have done in the way of human intercourse. It never occurred to me for a moment to go to my agent and say to him: Look here, I've come here, on your recommendation, to see life. You show it to me!

I was glad when the fortnight was over and I could with dignity go home again. Home felt better than it had felt for a long time—and *was* better too; for my literary success had won me the further privilege of a room of my own, where my third novel, *Spell Land*, had already been started. Hitherto, though the contents of my novels had been strictly private until publication, their writing had been as public as a street accident. I wrote them generally on the dining-room table, with all the business, pleasure and strife of the family surging round me. Housekeeping orders were given over my head, maids came in and out, visitors called, and all the time my pencil moved in response to a mind blissfully detached from all save its own expression. I confess, however, that latterly this detachment had begun to fail, partly, perhaps, because of my increasing age, principally, no doubt, because of my increasing sense of my own importance. I was a real author now, entitled to solitude, and two years after the publication of my first book I had it.

Was it a good gift? Certainly I have written better novels since then, but their appearance did not coincide with my withdrawal from the dining-room table. I am inclined to think that even lost me more than it gained, for the power of writing in the midst of bustle and racket is a gift of the gods which no pride of authorship really justified me in throwing away. Now I have gone so much to the opposite extreme that I am unable to write away from my own writing-desk, and even there the smallest distraction may break up a morning's work. I should find life easier if I had not once deliberately sensitized myself in the interests of my professional dignity.

2

My next visit to London was more successful than the first, for I did not spend it at the club in

Piccadilly, but at a boarding-house in South Kensington, inhabited mainly by students at the Royal College of Music. I owed this improvement to the officiousness of a friend of my mother's, who told her that for a girl of my age to stay alone at a club —even a ladies' club—was improper, and *that* was why none of the members had spoken to me. I should have resented this interference if I had not come independently to the conclusion that I did not want to go back there; and I had heard somehow of this boarding-house in Redcliffe Gardens.

It was a fortunate move, for I now really enjoyed visiting London. Every morning, after an eight o'clock breakfast, I set out for more exciting parts of the capital, returning in the evening to dine and talk with young women of my own age. I was also beginning to make literary friends. None of them was in the least eminent, but as till then I had not spoken to a single author, barring a writer of magazine stories whose manuscripts were occasionally accepted, I was grateful for the smallest poet or novelist.

One of these introduced me to my first real celebrity—Mrs. Alice Meynell. I spent one Sunday evening at her flat, and was profoundly shaken by

[75]

the experience. The atmosphere—artistic, cultured, casual—was entirely different from that of my own home, where Sunday supper meant the family sitting down in state to eat cold beef and prunes and talk about the evening's sermon. The lighting of the room, the numbers present, the way the company was always changing as people drifted in and out, the talk, the piano playing, the simple yet pleasant meal served in pottery bowls on polished oak instead of in china plates on a white cloth, produced in me a definite disquiet.

So that was how literary people lived, and that was what they looked like. They did not know how differently I lived, but they could see how differently I looked. The lovely, trailing dresses of the Miss Meynells made me dissatisfied with my clumsy coat and skirt and the white satin blouse that held my neck in a grip of whalebone. Evidently literary women did not wear whaleboned collars, and feeling that mine were wrong I cut them out of all my dresses. But even then I did not look like the Miss Meynells.

That did not, however, stop my collar-cutting, which I carried still further into abstract fields, cutting the collars off all my religious beliefs. For that evening had settled a growing conviction that literary people are not on the whole devout members of the Church of England. My hosts' Catholicism was at the time beyond my appreciation. I knew absolutely nothing of Catholicism except as a foreign religion I had just caught sight of abroad and as a bad end that Anglicans sometimes come to at home. I knew nothing of indigenous English Catholicism, and the expression of religion in the Meynell household was so artistically conditioned that it was thrown away on my present mood, which could not see the wood for the trees. I had had, on the other hand, a long, and to my mind, deeply intellectual conversation with an American visitor who guided me to the discovery that people go to church in response to a herd instinct from which great minds stand aloof.

3

First Edna Lyall, then the Meynells. . . . It says much for the perversity of my reactions that my two bouts of unbelief should have been inspired respectively by a devout Anglican and a household of charming Catholics. In each case I snatched hold of some totally irrelevant detail and hypnotized myself with it, though my second apostasy was more reasonably conditioned than the first. It was also much more willing. This time my faith was not suddenly plucked off me like a bird's feathers, but deliberately and decently discarded like unfashionable clothing. I had come to the conclusion that religion belonged to the period of writing at the dining-room table, and was even less compatible with my dignity as an author.

The sad thing is that I could now have been as High Church as I liked, for my emancipation had come with a rush and was now established in all spheres. But I no longer wanted to be High Church. I did not want to be an atheist—I had had enough of that at thirteen—but I wanted desperately to be Progressive and Enlightened. I wanted to be free of Outworn Dogmas and Threadbare Conventions, and I had little difficulty in casting them aside, because I wished to do so. Doubts based on reason and reflection came later, as I learned to rationalize my wish.

I am afraid it is quite impossible to make out of this episode a case of intellectual conviction or revolt. No more now than at thirteen, was I led by any mental discovery. I had simply yielded once again to suggestion—this time to the suggestion that orthodox religion is out of place and slightly ridiculous in a rising novelist. I had the will to disbelieve.

I at once began to justify this will by a course of reading that seemed to me daringly heterodox. I started with Nietzsche, who impressed me deeply—most of all, I think, by the fact of my reading him, my first anti-Christian philosopher. He certainly did not influence my life and thoughts apart from the suggestive power of certain phrases, and I had no intellectual grasp of his philosophy. Nor did I understand the nature of his protest against religion, grounded as it was in the protest of his ill-health against life itself, whereas my own was based rather in an ignorant, undirected appetite for life and experience.

Besides Nietzsche, I fed my unbelief on certain works of Biblical exegesis by various modernist scholars. The Bible had loomed large in my Anglican upbringing, and it is generally the first image a revolting Protestant seeks to overthrow. The reason is the same as that which makes the Priesthood the first attack of revolting Catholics—it represents authority. In the case of the Bible, no one is readier to furnish weapons of assault than the Protestants themselves. Eminent divines of the Church of England provided me with all the ammunition I required. Under their guidance I learned that the New Testament is no sacred collection of inspired books, but a fortuitous group of eccentrically edited documents—the editors of which were not unlike certain of their kind to-day in wresting facts to suit their religious and political convictions.

I emerged from this course of study without an illusion left. The Bible (or rather the authorized version) still existed as a source of magnificent prose, but as a guide to religion it was hopelessly disqualified. I do not suppose that the reverend writers had actually aimed at this effect, but that was how I reacted to their teaching.

I was now beginning to feel really free. Not that I had made any open breach with "organized religion"—my religious activities were as secret as my literary activities used to be—but I felt free and detached in my mind. If I still went to church I did so only to avoid argument; and in private I had given up the burden of prayer. Within certain bounds—bounds set by expediency—I did as I liked, and became very much happier and better tempered.

Charles Bradlaugh has spoken of the relief that comes when dogma is given up—a statement the truth of which lies in the fact that dogma is seldom given up while it is still living. A creed may become a corpse when love and zeal have ceased to inform it, and I was glad to lay down the dead body of what had once been a living faith. It was not I alone who had killed it—it might still have been alive if I had been allowed to feed and clothe it as my instincts dictated. But no matter what the cause or whose the blame, I had for some time been carrying a corpse around with me, and I was glad, infinitely glad, to lay down my burden.

Unfortunately my relief soon became tempered by a sense that something was missing. The religious side of my nature had always been well developed, and I could not be happy—at least, not at that time—without any religion at all. One form of religious expression had failed, but the need remained and sought to re-express itself.

This no doubt is why I began to read Emanuel Swedenborg. For anyone who has given up Anglicanism as dogmatic and credulous to turn to

Swedenborg is about as funny as for anyone who
finds the English climate too relaxing to go and
live in Singapore. It is now impossible for me to
recapture that lost attraction. The fact is, of course,
that I was hungry, and ready and able to swallow
stuff that would have nauseated me had my appetite been normally satisfied. With Swedenborg or
soon afterwards came Madame Blavatsky and a
motley crew of occultists and theosophists. "The
statements was tough, but interestin' " . . . I swallowed them all.

Such a diet could not fail to affect the novel I
was writing. I did not succeed in keeping my religious enthusiasms out of *Spell Land* as I succeeded
in keeping them out of later novels. There was a
governess in *Spell Land*, and I changed her into a
Swedenborgian minister. It was not a happy trans-
formation, for though like many characters, she
did better when I had changed her sex, a Swedenborgian minister is out of place in the Sussex weald,
and the doctrines which he enunciated cast an alien
shadow over the story. I do not mean that strange
religions are not believed and practised in Sussex,
or that to be a Swedenborgian is more unusual than
to be a Cokeler or an Elamite or a Beemanite or a

High Haldenite. But these latter religions are indigenous, local grown—their very eccentricity comes from the soil from which they spring; whereas Swedenborgianism comes from London and has a Germanic lucidity and neatness that accord badly with the muddled ways of the south.

Another drawback to *Spell Land* as a novel is that it is much too literary. I had been reading omnivorously for a number of years, beginning as a matter of conscience when I renounced Edna Lyall and the delightfully a-moral schoolgirl stories of L. T. Meade for a sober course of the classics. Since then I had chiefly hung round such masters as Richardson, Fielding, Sterne, Smollett, Jane Austen, Emily Brontë, George Borrow and William Blake. The effect of some of them on my own writing is obvious, though it is remarkable that those which have delighted me most, both then and since—Jane Austen and William Blake, whom I might call respectively my Bible and my hymn book—have had no discernible influence on my style at all. But George Borrow has left his mark on *The Tramping Methodist*, and the critics of *Starbrace* easily guessed my predilection for Field-

[83]

ing and his contemporaries, to say nothing of the *Newgate Calendar* and *Lives of the Highwaymen*.

But in *Spell Land* no guessing is required, for I myself supply the information. Not only are the pages sprinkled with titles—just as snobbish in their way as if I had taken them from Debrett—but my borgian minister quotes generously from the heroine is called Emily Branwell, the Sweden-sources of his belief, while the hero answers him from Nietzsche, and the general narrative is sprinkled with infatuating archaisms from Burton's *Anatomy of Melancholy*.

The critics were not slow to notice this development, and my reviews were not quite as good as for the two earlier novels. From them I gathered that though *Spell Land* was in many ways a more adult book than the first two—it stands outside the daydream category and has a modern setting—I had overloaded it with ideas that were not my own and were largely extraneous to the subject I had chosen.

4

For *Spell Land* I received an advance of forty pounds, ten pounds more than for *Starbrace*, and I spent the greater part of it on a trip to Paris. It proved a more expensive trip—to my parents—than I had reckoned, for while there I contracted pneumonia and came home only just in time for a six months' illness. I had never been really ill before, and the experience was the most disturbing I had had so far. I came out of it with an intense love of life and a feeling that much of my life had hitherto been wasted—that I had read, thought and dreamed too much and must now do something different. At the height of my illness, when death was more than a possibility, I had groped for religion, but had been unable to find it in the bed-side Communion Service that exhausted me and upset my family. As soon as I grew better I switched, not incomprehensibly, from another world to this.

I shall never forget those first days of convalescence, or the joy of renewed contacts with life—when a breath of spring air from the garden was enough to make me feel faint with ecstasy, and the sight of growing flowers or a star at twilight brought tears to my eyes. But as my health grew and I became once more familiar with the world outside my room, nature was not enough. I wanted the fullness of life in human experience—I wanted love.

My books seemed dull and arid—Swedenborg and the occultists became a cloud veiling something I no longer cared to see. I fretted secretly, because I felt that my youth was going by without bringing me anything worth remembering—my literary successes had lost their savour; besides, one can have that sort of thing when one is old.

I was twenty-four in actual years, about nineteen in looks, and not more than sixteen in experience. Apart from my three novels I was very young indeed. All girls at that time were younger, I think, than they are now, but I was younger than most of my contemporaries. I knew very few men, and with these my relations were founded mostly on talk—barring one or two silent and secret fallings in love that belonged emotionally to the schoolroom.

For a time I felt unhappy, but not for long. It has always been my experience that one has only to want a thing badly enough for it to happen sooner or later. I had wanted literary success, and it had come to me—largely through my own efforts. I wanted love-affairs, and they came to me—I will not say largely through my own efforts, but certainly not without some enterprise on my part.

I now began to take a great deal of trouble with my appearance. Hitherto, though I had dressed with desperate earnestness for certain occasions, such as my first visit to my publisher, I had in general spent very little thought or money on clothes. But now I began to study the fashions and to strain my resources in London dress shops. The ironmonger no longer supplied me with pale blue straw trimmed with pink rose-buds, nor the antediluvian tailor with the last leg-of-mutton sleeves in England. I remember a black and red spotted dress that was a success for years (a certain conservatism was forced on me by my finances) and the equally long-lived triumph of a dark grey coat and skirt worn with a cherry-coloured blouse and crowned with a cocked hat like a field-marshal's. No one had ever told me that women dress only to impress their own sex, or that "all men ask for is neatness and fashion"—two points on which, no doubt, I had done well to improve myself, even if the rest was wasted.

Now, though I still lived at home, I was definitely leading my own life. I had a number of friends, male and female, whom my parents had never met. They were unsuspicious and never troubled me with questions as to what I did in my absences, or drew any deductions from my changed appearance; and I was careful to tell them nothing, as I had well-founded doubts as to their reaction to my thrills. It must therefore have been a tremendous shock to them when one of my affairs burst, as it were, all over them, and they were suddenly brought up against a completely unknown young man threatening incoherently their daughter's life.

I shall never forget how splendidly they rose to the occasion; in fact I cannot help thinking that my father got a certain amount of kick out of it. We were staying in an hotel, and I can still see him trotting round the winter garden to arrange just where I was to take cover if my swain should arrive blazing away with his revolver—which of course he never did, contenting himself with fuliginous letters. I will not say that my father was disappointed.

As for me, it was my first real taste of sorrow. My love was not real by any standard that I have now, but the sorrow was, and for several weeks I felt almost broken-hearted. It was a young sorrow, and I kept a diary, which fortunately was lost, and wrote some verse which unfortunately was published. But it was a real sorrow all the same.

My fourth novel, *Isle of Thorns*, appeared soon afterwards. I had started it shortly after I finished *Spell Land*, but my illness had cut into it and delayed its progress for several months. It breaks new ground in more ways than one, for this time my publishers were not Messrs. George Bell & Sons, with whom I had been ever since my first novel, but the firm of Constable. My contract with Bell had ended and my agent and I both thought I should do better with a publisher with a larger novel list.

The scene of this novel is laid in a part of Sussex new to me—the Ashdown Forest district, some thirty miles from home. In those days I did not have to know a part of the country well in order to write about it—one visit and an ordinance survey map was enough. I had been taken to Nutley on my first motor-car drive. It seems odd to think this happened as late as 1910, but I cannot remember an earlier one. No doubt the momentousness of the occasion helped to impress the place on my imagination.

Isle of Thorns appeared in 1913. Seen from the angle of 1937, it has some good points, though it is, I think, in certain parts extremely silly. I had managed almost entirely to avoid the laboured bookishness of *Spell Land*, but I had not been able to keep out some rather painful vulgarities. The novel is more personal than any I had written hitherto, and the heroine is in many ways myself as I would have liked to be—my ambitions were then on the low side. It had a moderately good reception from a cooling press, and I think some of my friends were sorry I had written it; but it was a better book than the one that followed.

This story—*Three Against the World*—was written entirely under the weight of my recent experiments with life, and in a state of harassed and divided attention. Authorship had lost its gleam, which it had worn longer than religion, but which had faded at last—or rather had passed on to what I called Experience. *Three Against the World* is not only forced and unreal, but shows an astonishing poverty of invention, being simply a new

and enlarged edition of one of my schoolgirl novelettes—an effusion called *Tares of the Field*.

The reception by the critics was better than the
sales, which were lower than any I had hitherto
reached—only about five hundred. The book had
been published by Messrs. Chapman & Hall, for
Constable had not been pleased enough with the
sales of *Isle of Thorns* to give me the advance of
fifty pounds I asked for. Chapman & Hall paid the
advance and then politely showed me the door.
They were disappointed—they had hoped for better things. No, they did not want to see me and
they refused to give me a contract for my next
book.

For the first time since the acceptance of *The
Tramping Methodist* I found myself without a
publisher. I was in the street.

Chapter Four

A novel with a father—War, war-work,
war-time—Hard happiness—The rhymers
—The Escape to Sirius—Led by a star.

I

FOR many people my first novel is *Sussex Gorse*—
I often meet readers who have never heard of its
five struggling predecessors. The reason for this
does not lie in any remarkable sale or publicity—
the book appeared in the middle of the war and
sold no more than a thousand copies; nor were the
reviews much better than for *The Tramping Methodist*. But somehow it made an impression and has
been remembered only too well, for it still con-
tinues to be cast up at me as an example of what I
was able to do—once. It is also definitely the first
of a line of similar books; its literary relationship

[92]

to my best-known novel *Joanna Godden*, for instance, is much more obvious than that of its remoter ancestors.

To me the most remarkable thing about the book is how different it is from *Three Against the World*. Only two years divide the appearance of the two, and yet the first is certainly the worst novel I have written and the second possibly the best. A psychologist might like to know what had happened to me in the interval, for there are other differences. One novel is subjective and romantic in outlook, the other is objective and realistic; one is artificial and the other natural; one is immature in its portrayal of life and character, the other—though crude in places and inclined to see events and characters larger than life—is written from a definitely adult point of view. Had anything happened to account for this change?

The answer is a simple one. I had met somebody who had influenced me for the better both as a writer and as a human being. Anyone more different from myself in either respect it would be hard to find. W. L. George was a Frenchman lately come to England who had attracted the public attention with three novels, the first of which—a realistic and unsentimental study of prostitution—had achieved the publicity of a library ban, though it would scarcely startle anybody now.

He was a man of extraordinary vitality and intelligence, and everything he wrote was alive—even his faults were challenging. *The Making of an Englishman* and *The Second Blooming* are novels that should not have been forgotten—if indeed they are forgotten. But some time before his early death, Willy George committed a sort of literary suicide. He had always taken a cynical view of himself as a writer—"I do it only because it's the pleasantest way I know of making a living." A war novel he wrote from his heart had a bad reception, and that helped his decision to write only to sell. Of course, such a decision was fatal, for no best seller was ever written of malice aforethought, and all Willy succeeded in doing was to kick himself down further in the critics' estimation. But at the time I first met him he was at the height of his new success, and I know that he would have made a real mark on literature if he had not suffered from that rare fault—a too-ready contempt of his own powers.

But though he misjudged himself, he judged me with a candour and a generosity that were my literary salvation. I owe it to him if I have written anything worth reading. He had read *Three Against the World*, and he had seen its faults, and much more remarkably its possibilities. He had also read *Spell Land* and decided that it was on the lines of that novel that I would produce by best work.

"In *Spell Land* you have made the place your most important character—the idea doesn't come out clearly enough, but it's there. Also, in *Spell Land* you have written about country people. Your people in *Isle of Thorns* and *Three Against the World* are just townspeople living in the country, which isn't half such a good thing. Anyone can write that sort of book, but you can write something better."

I told him about the new novel I had begun. It was called *Green Apple Harvest*, but it bore no resemblance to the novel that appeared six years later under that name; and it was about townspeople living in the country. He was not pleased with the idea, and discouraged me so effectively that I scrapped it. But his criticism was not all destructive. "Look here," he said, "I've got a novel for you. Why not write about a man who reclaims and cultivates a wild piece of moorland—sacrifices everything to it and succeeds in the end? . . . the piece of land must dominate the story, which must be grim and savage. You might call it *Sussex Oak*."

We were standing on the platform of Hampstead Tube Station, and the book seemed already written. My only protest was a small one—the title had been used before.

"Never mind—then call it *Sussex Gorse*. That'll be even better, for the old lady subscribers at the library will think it such a pretty name and feel it's sure to be a pretty story. I see it as something on the lines of Zola's *La Terre*. It is going to be your great book."

Later on he sent me two pages of suggestions—ideas—characters—historical scenes to be incorporated. We talked over the plan, and I cannot remember whether it was he or I who thought of the name of the hero, Reuben Backfield. I was still a sentimentalist and wanted to end the story on a note of regret, but he insisted that Backfield must find his sacrifices worth while. "I don't see the story ending tragically. He got what he wanted. He didn't care for the things he gave up as much as he cared for the place he gave them up for—

or he wouldn't have given them up. He was a strong man and he wouldn't regret anything."

So I owe to W. L. George not only the structure of *Sussex Gorse*, but the fact that it did not end on a false note. Another thing I owe to him was the ease with which I wrote it. Not that he helped me at all with the actual writing; we scarcely mentioned the book once it had been started—I am one of those writers who are constitutionally unable to discuss any work in progress, and he had no wish for a collaboration. But he gave me a new technique of writing—a technique which has saved me months of work and worry.

Hitherto my plan had been to sit down with a pencil, a penny exercise book and a general idea of the story I wanted to write—begin writing and go on writing till I stuck. Then I would struggle somehow through the obstacle and write on till the next, then on and on till the first draft was finished. Then I would write a second and final draft which involved practically the re-writing of the whole story. On Willy's advice I wrote only one draft, after having first made a very elaborate and detailed plan—"know exactly what you're going to write before you begin. Plan it even down to paragraphs." I have followed this method ever since, and practise has made it increasingly easy. Formerly I could not write a novel of eighty to ninety thousand words in less than a year. *Sussex Gorse*, which runs to nearly a hundred and fifty thousand words, took me six months, and all my subsequent novels have been written in periods varying from four months to nine. Speed is not, of course, the author's best friend, but in this case, I think, it definitely improved the quality of my writing. A novel which has been too much worked over often goes flat, and no amount of laborious revision can take the place of careful planning beforehand.

Having given me an idea for a novel and taught me writing without tears, Willy George completed his work by finding me a publisher. I was of course at that time without one, and I doubt if I should have managed to write *Sussex Gorse* on the doorstep of hope. As it happened I wrote it on a "firm" contract with Messrs. Nisbet. I who six months ago had been uncertain whom I could turn to with my next novel, actually wrote it in the certainty—enjoyed for the first time—that it would be published. The fact that it was not published till nearly two years later is due to my also writing for the same publishers a small book on Galsworthy and to the outbreak of war.

2

For about a week before and a week after war was declared I think that most writers imagined their work was done for. It seemed impossible that anything so frail as one's imagination could survive in such a storm. Before long, however, the cry of other tradesmen—Business as Usual—proved to be no vain boast (or prayer). We found that writing and publishing would go on much the same; in fact the war seemed to give an urge to literature, especially to the more sensitive and imaginative kinds. Never before in modern times had poetry such a vogue—poets were actually able to publish at their publishers' expense, and there is a rumour that some of them even received royalties. The great complex of violence, hate, lust, cunning, fear and other primitive emotions released by the explosion of war also dragged up from the bottom of our hearts the primitive urges of poetry and religion. Poets sang and people prayed—till the

[99]

war ended, and poetry and prayer were bundled away and suppressed with uglier things.

At first I reacted to the war in much the same way as the War Office; that is to say I saw it in the terms of South Africa in 1899. Schoolgirl memories revived and asked naïvely to be repeated—Dolly Grey, Bluebell, the Absent-Minded Beggar and rows of patriotic buttons round my hat. It was an infantile reaction, but more harmless in me than at Whitehall.

I recovered from it fairly quickly. At first, of course, we all thought that peace was bound to come in a few months; and most civilians found an escape from the realities of Mons and the Marne in a dream of Russians pouring their countless hordes into France by way of every town and village in Britain. But when winter came and the tired armies settled down into the mud and the Principal Boys in all the pantomimes sang "Tipperary," some of us began to wake up and feel ashamed. Personally I felt guilty till the end of the war.

Emotionally speaking, I had an uneasy time. After the first few months I could not join in the singing and hating, or believe in British propaganda or in the fact so obvious to the rest of the country that anyone with a German sounding name must be a spy. I could have smacked the distributors of white feathers, and such posters as "Is your Best Boy in Khaki?" made me hot with shame. On the other hand I could not feel at ease with the definitely pacifist groups or with the Conscientious Objectors. In more than one case I suspected that conscience was only a rationalizing of a natural but unpopular objection to being maimed or killed, and I respected the few who were brave enough to state their objection in those terms. I also respected the large number who went, many of them already disillusioned, to suffer and die *with* humanity, though they could no longer feel they were dying *for* it— who refused to stand apart from the great woe either with or without a garment of righteousness.

I did a certain amount of war-work—I made swabs and bandages, I sold tea and doughnuts in a canteen, I added to the muddle of a War-Office department. But unlike so many writers at that period I was never really absorbed in the war or distracted by it—doubtless for the reason that I had been spared the fate of most of the women of England, and never had anyone I really and truly cared for out at the front. I was brotherless, my father was over seventy, and my best boy was not in khaki. So my attention was not forcibly dragged away from my literary work and fixed on some dark, imagined place overseas, held there by irregularly frequent buff envelopes, and then suddenly twisted out and knotted into a few hours of agonized happiness called leave. My heart was in England and available for the writing of *Sussex Gorse*.

I enjoyed writing it, for it was an escape from the turmoil and unhappiness round me, and once more I took a definite pride and pleasure in my work. I will not say that writing once more wore a gleam, for the days were passing when my interests must be like fairy queens in pantomime, with stars on their heads. But I enjoyed the ease and simplicity of my new technique—my imagination, unhampered by external difficulties, had a freer and deeper play than in any of the earlier books. Also, inspired by the novel's father, I thought less about the importance and glory of authorship and more about the fun and interest of ordinary human life.

The result was not a complete success, for I was not yet quite a realist. Though I now did my best to see life honestly I still saw it through the enlarging spectacles of romance. The critics were not slow to spot the fundamental weaknesses of *Sussex Gorse*—the fact that it is too big to be true. Reuben Backfield is too consistent in his ruthlessness to be quite human, and there is something mechanical rather than inevitable in the misfortunes of his family. Willy George was disappointed in my treatment of the idea he had given me. He found it without shape or proportion and drew me a diagram of the way it should have been done. I am not sure that he was right about this—the book might easily have been spoilt by too much designing.

I myself thought well of *Sussex Gorse* and was desperately anxious for it to succeed. Its reception did not disappoint me. Examined in detail, it does not look too wonderful, but the general result was gratifying. Apart from the reviews and a good deal of praise from those whose opinion I valued, I knew that the novel was being talked about. I felt a change towards myself in literary places, and knew that in a measure I had "arrived," though the critics still talked of Promise and the book which I would write one day—and have never

written. As for the sales, I had never before sold
more than a few hundred copies, and a thousand
was respectable compared with some earlier figures.
Besides, as my publisher never ceased reminding
me, there was a war on.

That was the way things happened in England—
in America they did not happen quite so well.
Strangely enough *Three Against the World* had
been the first of my novels to find a publisher in
the United States. I was disappointed, and I confess, surprised when the same publisher declined
Sussex Gorse. For several years it seemed to be a
rule that the New York publisher of any one of
my novels should decline the next. Messrs. Dutton
published *Three Against the World* and declined
Sussex Gorse, which found a home with Messrs.
Knopf, who rejected *The Challenge to Sirius*,
which went back to Messrs. Dutton, who threw
out *Little England*, which was published by Messrs.
Doran, who returned me to Messrs. Dutton with
Tamarisk Town. It was not till then that I found
that solid, almost matrimonial security of publication that I have enjoyed in England ever since
1916.

CHAPTER FOUR

3

I remember the few weeks following the publication of *Sussex Gorse* as some of the happiest in my life, though the happiness was, as I realized almost immediately afterwards and half realized at the time, of a hard, brittle kind, that suddenly, for no apparent reason, dissolved into dust. It was of course without any background or setting in the world around me—a small, frail, personal possession that I enjoyed only because I was able to shut my eyes to so much misery, so much fear, so much wickedness. . . . But though the best of life might be tumbling round me in those first weeks of 1916 I was able for a short time to concentrate on my own little piece of private fortune. I was more successful than I had ever been before, more proud, more popular. I had several delightful friends—no longer exclusively among the hangers-on of literature, but among its established practitioners. Except for the smallness of my sales—and I had never had any definite ambitions as a best seller—I had seen my girlhood's hopes fulfilled. *Sussex Gorse* was just the sort of a novel I had always wanted to write, and its success was just the sort of success I told myself I wanted—not too blatant or indiscriminate to be secure.

The only drawback was that I had so very little money. I had been given fifty pounds in advance for *Sussex Gorse*, and as the advance was never earned I received no more, except a few pounds for the sale of the "sheets" in America. In actual spending value that fifty pounds was probably as little as the twenty pounds I was paid for *The Tramping Methodist*. Moreover, my parents—hit by falling dividends and soaring prices—found it necessary to reduce the dress allowance that for the last six or seven years had supplemented whatever I could make out of literature.

My success with *Sussex Gorse* had not made me any richer, though it had greatly increased my expenses. My improved literary position had more than ever inclined me for London, and I was also determined to dress the part of a successful lady novelist. As I could not afford to buy clothes I made them myself, though I had not even the most elementary knowledge of dressmaking. I took my measurements by the simple process of lying down on the material and cutting it out round me with a pair of nail scissors. I cannot now think that the results were as successful as I thought them at the time.

London was a magnet that drew me, as it drew most of the nation; though as I remember it then I wonder how I or anyone could have endured it in those days. I remember it as noise and darkness and aching restlessness, with the night coming down over the shaded street-lamps, and endless crowds moving to and fro, anxious, exhausted, overworked and overwrought, yet at that evening time all seemingly bent on pleasure. . . . Let us crown ourselves with rosebuds before they be withered. . . . Let us eat and drink, for to-morrow we die. We were all trying desperately to forget the shadow of death lying over us—the shadow of the leave train, of the guns, of the Gothas; none of us, whether soldier or civilian, was outside that shadow, and sometimes it seemed as if we were all prowling the streets together because we could not sit still under it. But at least in London we could see the dark wings move—we could watch our doom in a way that was impossible in the black, deserted streets of the Provincial towns, where all was guessing and silence. In London there was always an uneasy mutter of voices, and sometimes one heard a voice that sounded like the truth . . . that was why some of us were always going to London, even when work and friendship did not call us there.

I spent a certain amount of time in the country, too—walking and cycling through a strangely empty and strangely prosperous land. Everywhere the fields were worked and trim, and the cottages had white lace curtains in the windows instead of a thickness of musk and geraniums. Everywhere was an entirely new air of comfort. The farmer and the agricultural labourer were enjoying their brief prosperity, as for the first and last time in two generations the nation came to depend on them in the manner of the past. Wages went up from fifteen to forty-five shillings a week, the price of wheat rose to ninety shillings a quarter, under-wood was sold at as much as sixty pounds a cant. It was a brief, golden age for those left to enjoy it.

But my heart was not in the country as it used to be. The complex of war runs to herds and crowds, and my imagination was busy with a town. For the first time I was planning a book that should be entirely urban. The idea had come to me with a dream. I dreamed one night that I walked up to a high, narrow, red-fronted house in a Hastings street, and going in at the door and up the stairs I found myself in a small back bedroom. It was sparely furnished, but I remember a counterpane in soft, glowing colours on a narrow bed, and a pleasant outlook over trees. As I entered the room I experienced a wonderful sensation of release and fulfilment—all the uneasiness and struggle of life in war-time were gone, and my own personal anxieties had ended in deep content. For days I wandered about the streets of old Hastings looking for the house of my dream. I never found it, but I found instead on Tamarisk Steps the idea for a novel called *Tamarisk Town.*

> Show me the town they saw
> Withouten fleck or flaw—
>   Aflame, more fine than glass
> Of fair Abbayes the boast,
> More glad than wax of cost
>   Doth make at Candlemass
> The lifting of the Host. . . .

These lines of Digby Mackworth Dolben's[1] were at the back of *Tamarisk Town* and sustained it in the shining atmosphere that clothed the old

[1] *The Poems of Digby Mackworth Dolben,* edited with a Memoir by Robert Bridges (Oxford University Press).

fishing-quarter of Hastings while I was writing the first part. I had come across Dolben at the same time as I first read Rupert Brooke. They were my personal share of that new love of poetry which was sweeping the war-sick nation. Brooke was a contagion due to the times, and I doubt if I have read a line of him since the war ended. Dolben, though an inferior poet, has stayed with me longer. His double strain of classicism and Catholicism, fatalism and romance, appeal still as they appealed then to a mind always conscious of the shadows cast by its illumination.

> Where many knights and dames
> With new and wondrous names
>   One great Laudaté Psalm
> Go singing down the street.
> 'Tis peace upon their feet—
>   In hand 'tis pilgrim palm
> Of Goddes Land so sweet. . . .

The exquisite medievalism of *He would have his Ladye Sing*—which Robert Bridges has compared to the coloured light of a stained glass window—enchanted me as I walked through the red and black streets of Tamarisk Town. But out in the lanes and fields beyond Bodlestreet and Redpale,

among the pinewoods of Ashburnham, already rav-
aged for war, I had ringing in my ears a darker
strain.

> There is neither fast nor feast,
> None is greatest, none is least;
> Times and orders all have ceased.
> There the bay-leaf is not seen;
> Clean is foul and foul is clean;
> Shame and glory these have been,
>   But shall not be.

> When we pass away in fire,
> What is found beyond the pyre?
> Sleep, the end of all desire.
> Lo, for this the heroes fought;
> This the gem the merchant bought,
> This the seal of laboured thought
>   And subtilty.

Only a Christian could have written this heavily
stressed Paganism, and no one who was not fundamentally a Christian could have found comfort in
it. The dark rhymes soothed me as they sang themselves in my head; I found them more assuaging
to grief than any thoughts of:

> Him who sitteth there,
> The Christ of purple hair,
> And great eyes deep with ruth.

My head was in that unhappy summer of 1916 a mass of jingling, juggling lines. Some were from the poets, as I have quoted; others were from the Pierrots on the Pier. . . .

> Next morning when the fambly had their breakfusses
> Little Fido's face was absent from the board,
> And the servant said: "Oh, Missus, I expectusses
> Pore Fido's gone to goodness, thank the Lord!" . . .

I was like a child running about with a bell—every sort of ting-a-ling to deafen me to my own thoughts. . . . "And when I told them how beautiful you were, they wouldn't believe me." . . . "You called me baby-doll a year ago." . . . "It was the ragpicker, the ragpicker." . . . In the end my head became so full of misery and rhymes that I could not go on writing *Tamarisk Town*. I had written Part I, I had struggled to the end of Part II. Then I gave it up; I could write no more. I must change everything about me, even the novel I am writing. I must escape.

4

Luckily for myself if not for my readers I have never torn up a manuscript. I have put several novels aside, but destroyed none of them, and in fact have revived and finished all of them except one. *Tamarisk Town*, and two later novels—*The George and the Crown* and *Superstition Corner*—were all once given up for dead. I wrote and published two complete novels before I dug up and finished the buried *Tamarisk Town*.

The first of these, *The Challenge to Sirius*, is definitely a novel of escape. I wanted to escape—to get away. I said to myself: I must go to America. I don't know why America came into my mind just then, except that it is on the other side of the world. Of course to go there at that time was physically and financially impossible, but very shortly I came to see that I could go there in a novel. I could write a novel of which at least a part of the action should take place in America. My recklessness in leaving a background familiar to me since childhood for one I had never seen and of which I knew almost nothing was tempered by the decision to push my story back into historical times —the times of the Confederate War. I was always happy on historical ground, and I had perhaps an over-optimistic view of my powers to assimilate a new atmosphere.

But though *The Challenge to Sirius* is a novel of

escape, it also touches actuality more closely than any of my previous novels. It is, in fact, indirectly a war novel. My description of the American Civil War of 1861 is largely conditioned by my reactions to the European War of 1916. I was beginning to find it impossible to ignore the war entirely —as I had hitherto done and as most writers were urged by their publishers to do. On the other hand, the war was too close for direct transmission—I had to stand away from it somehow, and by stepping back some sixty years I was able to relieve that part of me which sought not escape but expression.

I wrote *The Challenge to Sirius* during the bitterly cold winter of 1917, when Canadian soldiers were snowballing in the streets of Hastings and comparing the climate of the English Riviera adversely with that of their home towns in Ontario and Saskatchewan. When I had finished it I went back to London and worked for about six months in the Army List department of the War Office.

While there I felt moved to go over some of the ground I had covered in my novel. The Army List department was then housed in Kingsway, and my lunch hour generally took me through Staple Inn into Holborn. It struck me that I had never been inside St. Alban's, Holborn, the church that played such an important part in the Oxford Movement and that is referred to more than once in *The Challenge to Sirius*.

The second part of that novel is staged in the literary London of the eighteen-fifties, and the hero, while experimenting in novel-writing, earns his living as a reporter for a newspaper started specially to oppose the spread of Ritualism. I had enjoyed writing about the early days of the Oxford Movement—chiefly because I felt that I was breaking new ground, for I no longer had any personal interest in the matter. I had drawn my facts mainly from documents (current histories, reports of law cases, etc.) and had little or no first hand knowledge of the churches that had led the revival —St. Paul's, Knightsbridge, St. George's-in-the-East, St. Alban's, Holborn.

Though I had done my best as a girl to be High Church, I knew very little about Anglo-Catholicism in its modern extremes, and the interior of St. Alban's, with its holy-water stoups, Sanctuary lights, Sacrament Chapel and praying women was a revelation to me. I had come out of a purely detached interest to see a place I had written about without seeing it, as I had written about the United States and Yucatan; but I came away in a very different mood. I was surprised—disturbed—even upset. For I had expected to see something that was as dead as Queen Victoria, a mere matter of literary interest. Instead of which I had found something which was living, moving, praying . . . the experience was about as much of a shock as to see a living face inside an ornamental suit of armour.

Having kept away for so long from all but the most occasional and perfunctory religious observances, I had like so many unbelievers supported myself with a convention—the convention that religion is static, dead and bound. I cannot tell by what faculty I saw that here it was alive; I suppose that I had not lost the power of recognizing prayer when I saw it, even though I no longer prayed. Certainly I felt that I had found something—something both alluring and disturbing, something that would not let me go away unless I promised to come back.

At first I came back only to the empty church— empty, that is, of any formal rite, for there were always people at prayer, mostly business girls like myself, kneeling at the back with their attaché cases beside them. I knelt too, and because I was ashamed to be silent and had no words of my own I bought a Prayer Book—not the Book of Common Prayer, but a twopenny manual better adapted to the church I used it in. In it I found the Hail Mary and the Litany of Loretto, and as I read them it crossed my mind to wonder if—supposing I ever meant to practise religion again—I had not better do it thoroughly as a Roman Catholic. Before I went further—supposing I ever should go further —would it not be wise to investigate the church which was the model if not the goal of the Anglo-Catholic movement?

Half-yielding to this suggestion I went one Sunday to Mass at St. James's, Spanish Place. The atmosphere seemed strangely desiccated. I was quite unused to austerity in religion, for even the simplest services of the Church of England are not austere—there is a glow of sentiment about them which no plainness of setting or detail can extinguish. Though I did not know it, my whole idea of religion was sentimental, and I could not adapt myself to any other conception. I was disappointed in the Catholic Church—or rather, in St. James's,

Spanish Place, for I investigated no further. I had expected something much more impressive.

The next Sunday I went to St. Alban's and found a very different—and to my mind, very superior—state of things. The morning service took the form of a luxurious High Mass, such as was usual in most Anglo-Catholic churches, even during the war. Though it was all very much more "extreme" than anything I had hitherto encountered, I immediately felt at home. Here was the right atmosphere for religion—warm, living, splendid, slightly exotic . . . I liked that foreign touch on my reviving associations. Something very deep in my heart was stirred, as it had not been stirred in the Catholic church. From very far off I lifted up my eyes and looked towards home.

Chapter Five

A long, nervous book—Map of the way home—Gunfire on the air—The bells of peace—Happiness is not enough—*Tamarisk Town* holds a secret—I preach the Gospel in *Green Apple Harvest*—The birth of *Joanna Godden*.

I

WHEN *The Challenge to Sirius* appeared, England was in the depths of war-time scarcity. Paper was difficult to obtain, newspapers were rationed and reviews were necessarily scanty. It was therefore inevitable that the book should receive less attention than *Sussex Gorse*, and it is difficult to say what the reception would have been had things been equal. As they were, I had no true standard of comparison.

[119]

But I do not think that even in similar circumstances, *The Challenge to Sirius* would have done as well as *Sussex Gorse*. It is a long, nervous, chaotic book, aiming at the sky but seldom hitting anything higher than a tree. For half of it I moved against a strange background, greatly to my own embarrassment. After the American Civil War the hero travels to Yucatan, of which—not surprisingly —I knew nothing, choosing it only because of the strong probability that the majority of readers must share my ignorance. Inevitably, both here and in the American scenes, the background weighs upon the author's consciousness, and the characters as a result are crushed flat. Character-drawing was almost the last grace to come to me as a writer, but it had already shown itself in *Sussex Gorse*— in *The Challenge to Sirius* it is driven back by stress of scenery and philosophy.

For *The Challenge to Sirius* makes a definite attempt to present a philosophy of life. It is not a new or a profound philosophy, but it is sincere in that it expresses a personal struggle. The remote star becomes the symbol of divine indifference, and one man's reaction to that overwhelming remoteness is the subject of the book. Though written primarily as an escape, it yet expresses more of myself—at a certain period—than any other novel. There never was a time when I had felt more remote from God. Yet there are signs in the book that I was already on the way back to Him . . . I had turned round—I was looking in His direction, even though I saw Him as nothing but a far-off, indifferent star.

If this is so, then my turning-point was not that visit to the church in Holborn, nor was that visit so detached and literary as I had thought, but engineered by a hidden desire which had already expressed itself in the novel. I cannot be sure of this— all I can see is that while writing the book I must have at least been dimly conscious once more of *direction*, though it was no more than the direction of a look. From a great distance I also saw the two forms of religion that were to be successively the path of my return. The first part of the story deals, as I have said, with the early days of the Tractarian movement in London, and the last gives a picture of Catholicism in Yucatan. My picture of Tractarianism is well-informed but hardly sympathetic; my picture of Catholicism is sympathetic but less well-informed. I certainly did not envisage myself as an adherent of either, but both had attracted my interest, the latter for the first time.

My dealings with tropical Catholicism rather worried my literary agent. I had not disguised—in fact, had overstressed—the drawbacks of bush religion. My priest was immoral, and his doctrine garbled with paganism; my agent was nervous—"it's always rash to offend the Church of Rome." In vain I pointed out to him that my study was sympathetic, that I had given Romanism at its worst the advantage over Anglicanism at its best. He was uneasy, though I do not exactly know what form he thought the Church's resentment would take—whether he expected the Inquisition to spirit me away, or my book to be crushed by some pontifical decree. Actually all that happened was that a Jesuit priest, reading it down in Sussex, marked me as one who should and possibly would join the Catholic Church—though his penetration can scarcely have gone as far as the day when he himself received me into it.

2

By the time the novel appeared I was back in Hastings, listening to the sound of the guns that

rumbled unceasingly over the Sussex weald, sometimes a definite roar, sometimes a mere pulse and
mutter on the air. It was those guns that gave me
the subject of my next book, *Little England*. I had
now, from a literary point of view, come abreast
of the war (I calculate that it takes about four
years for an outside event to reach that part of
me which turns life into literature), and I wanted
to write about it—directly—no longer at a distance
of sixty years. I had neither the wish nor the
knowledge to write about it in France, so I wrote
about it in England, and in the part of England
specially close and dear to me.

Every author, I am told, has a book which he
considers the public has not sufficiently appreci-
ated. If I am to put myself in that position, *Little
England* is that book. It came after two "big" ones,
and I find that if you want to make an impression,
you must draw your picture larger than life.
Reuben Backfield in *Sussex Gorse* and his successors in *Green Apple Harvest* and *Joanna Godden* are all something in the nature of Brocken
Spectres—they lie huge and impressive on a cloud,
and it is not till afterwards that the reader remem-
bers they were a little unreal in their poses, a little

blurred in their outlines. Characters like the Beatup family in *Little England* are if anything smaller than life is supposed to be. As one reviewer said, "The author means well, but writes only of commonplace people."

The explanation, however, does not lie entirely in the book itself, but also in the time of its appearance. That must share the responsibility for the small impression that it made. It was a war book and when it had been out only a very short time the war ended; and the war was no sooner ended than desperate efforts were made to forget it. War books were swept off the library shelves, and the rumour went round that publishers were inserting clauses in their contracts to prevent them being written; certainly none of any importance appeared for several years. The general and natural desire was to get back to normal life—to dig a deep grave for the past, build a comfortable house for the present and blow an idealistic bubble for the future.

As for me, I bore the times no grudge—they were good times. I had no one I loved at the front, but I do not think I have ever experienced a sweeter, more fundamental relief than that which came to me when the bells rang out on the signing of the Armistice. The world seemed to have begun again.

And yet the past year had not been a bad one for me personally. Much of it had been extremely happy; it was only that the nightmare of war and war conditions had become so overwhelming that any personal happiness was rather like a picnic on the edge of an abyss. The story of the last year of war is simple from a literary point of view, and I have come rather quickly to the end of it. But the main interest of 1918 for me is not literary, but religious. Ever since my return from London I had been aware of a change of direction—of focus, of accent, of axis . . . call it what you like. My mind was now pointing away from its former horizons, looking towards others which I had not seen since I was a girl at school.

This new orientation was inevitably associated with Anglo-Catholicism, which has been called (I forget by whom) the London, Brighton and South Coast religion, so that in leaving London for Hastings I was not leaving it behind me. It had been established at Christ Church, St. Leonards, for nearly three-quarters of a century, and as a schoolgirl I had made desperate, abortive efforts to attach myself to it there. I remember bolting down the street during an interval between classes, into the refuge of its warm, incense-smelling shadows, full of winking red lights—its atmosphere was always ten times more Catholic than that of any Catholic church I know. But it was thought subversive by my parents, and all I could do for myself—since my conscience would not tolerate an indefinite number of these escapes—was to wring from them the permission to go there three times before I gave it up for ever. I went twice, but kept the third time in reserve, as if it had been my last shilling. It was still unspent when I started going there regularly during the last year of the war.

I was pleased to find there everything that had attracted me at St. Alban's, Holborn. "Everything" does not mean only good music and a splendid ritual, but also a living faith. Anglican churches were not so empty during the war as they have become since, but even in 1918 the keen and crowded congregations at Christ Church were exceptional and inspiring. The preaching was of a high order and I began to learn something about the Catholic religion as practised in the Church of England.

[126]

CHAPTER FIVE

Doctrinally and philosophically my mind was still open. It may seem surprising that I should begin to attend a church before I had any serious thoughts of practising or believing the religion taught there. But such an inversion is not uncommon—in fact, I should say that in the majority of conversions the cart comes before the horse. "*À force de prendre l'eau bénite on devient croyant*" is how Pascal puts it.

I was now no longer satisfied with looking—I had begun to move. Uncertainly and half reluctantly I was groping my way to a light I saw ahead of me. Sirius no longer hung in the remote heavens, symbol of the divine indifference, but had become a sanctuary lamp, burning before the Altar of God. I approached this Altar in response to an instinct as fundamental and compelling as any that ever drove man and woman together. As a child that instinct had been thwarted and misdirected by well-meaning elders, and later on I had myself done all I could to suppress it, under the compulsion of a false shame. But now that at last I was aware of all the unhappiness which this brought, I wanted desperately to put things right again.

I knew now—or almost knew—that I could not be happy without religion. The trouble was that I was still in many ways very ignorant and prejudiced. I should have saved myself an enormous amount of trouble, delay and risk if I had not been so childishly put off by the outward severity of Catholicism. I cannot believe that it was the divine intention that I should spend twelve years as a sort of synthetic Catholic in the Church of England, though I acknowledge that the divine power has overruled the evil of my choice for good, which encourages me to think that that choice was not entirely silly and selfish. It was conditioned largely by the circumstances of my education and by the fact that from the time I was old enough to distinguish one form of religion from another, a sort of glamour had hung over the High Church movement. At school all the most popular girls and mistresses had been High Church (Oh, the Friday smell of fish cooking for the boarders' dinner! coupled with the knowledge that I myself must inevitably go home to Protestant beef or mutton), and my parents had added their disapproval to its attractions. Later on there had been that battle which I had lost, but the field of which had meanwhile been given up to me by the retirement of the conquering hosts. All the glamour of early associations and early enthusiasms was on the side of Anglo-Catholicism, whereas the unhyphenated kind was bound up with the peculiarities of unpopular French maids and my own abortive investigations.

It was no part of my problem now. My problem was based on the simple question—did I or did I not want to practise religion again? If I did, then the Anglo-Catholic religion was the only one I seriously thought of. Catholicism and ordinary Anglicanism were equally out of the picture. It never occurred to me to compromise with agnosticism by accepting a modernistic interpretation of Christianity—I do not think it often does. "Wistful agnostics" are much more prone ultimately to satisfy their cravings with a bellyful of some authoritative religion than with the carefully specialized and selected diet of the Modern Churchman's Union.

Besides, my agnosticism was not really a serious barrier between me and the acceptance of any creed. It must be remembered that I had originally acquired it through my own efforts—I had jockeyed myself out of Christianity as deliberately and artificially as anyone could be supposed to be jockeyed into it. I had never been overwhelmed with genuine doubt; my doubts had all been cultivated, and it would not be difficult to uproot what I myself had planted. I do not mean that I did not still see the case against Christianity—in fact, I probably saw it more clearly than I had seen it ten years earlier—but I now allowed myself to look at the other side, and the case appeared, if not better, at least as good. Intellectually it seemed that I had a free choice; but any really free and complete choice is made with the whole personality, not with the intellect alone. "Faith is the substance of things hoped for"—it is belief with the will (not to be confused with the mere will to believe). Therefore my problem was ultimately not a problem of the intellect but of the will—how much did I *want* religion?

I had a feeling that if I returned to it, the action would be final—I should not be able to withdraw again. And I was not so blinded by the glamour of Anglo-Catholicism that I failed to see the obligations. I should once again have to shoulder a burden that I had already found too heavy. Certainly I had no illusions . . . nor was I looking for a dope. Religion may be used as a drug, just as sex or science or art may be; but if ever I had needed that sort of escape it was at the time I turned away from it, not when I found myself turning back again. I then had nothing to run away from—in fact, my personal, private life was happier and more successful than it had been for a long time.

But it was this very happiness that showed me my need. I had once said to myself: if only I had this and that my life would be complete. Now I had them and it was not. There is, of course, nothing new in this discovery. "Thou hast made us for Thyself and our heart can never rest until it rest in Thee." . . . St. Augustine was only expressing what was already old in his day. "My soul thirsteth for Thee, my soul also longeth after Thee" . . . the psalmist was only echoing what thousands and millions had found out since the beginning of the world. The majority of human beings do not turn to God because they have not enough happiness but because happiness is not enough.

As for the corporate misery of the world in wartime, which I had often felt so keenly, that had no part in driving me back to religion, because actually I was unable to make any decision about it till the cloud had been lifted and the war was over. It was not till that moment of intense relief and happiness that my shifting desires suddenly hardened into the form of resolution. I made up my mind. I would. What was more, I must.

That sense of compulsion was with me almost from the signing of the Armistice. I knew that I should have to do it. The only questions were How and When. The How was the normal method of a Catholic's return to religion—that is to say, confession; the When was as soon as I could screw up the courage. Actually I made my first confession in the Church of England just before the Christmas of 1918. I was fortunate in having no idea of the risks I ran; I knew nothing of the troubles that may befall the layman who seeks the skilled ministrations of an untrained clergy.

"Will those fellows who are commonly called tough nuts to crack kindly not come to confession just before the Midnight Mass begins." This entreaty (made in a Sussex church one Christmas by a foreign priest) would be unnecessary in the Church of England, whose confessors have very little to do with tough nuts. Their practice is mostly among the devout, and their outlook in consequence is sometimes narrow. The only attempt I know on the part of an Anglican tough nut—and not so very tough, either—to "receive the benefit of absolution" resulted in a shocked and angry clergyman telling him that as it was his first confession he would give him absolution *this time*. He never went again.

So I see that I was lucky; or perhaps I should say that God was good, and guided me to someone who, though like all Anglican confessors entirely self-taught, was learned in the ways of God and man. I shall always be grateful to him and to the system that produced him and so much else that was good. I myself was very ignorant, and my confession was defective in almost every way save that of intention. But it had (apart from other considerations) the psychological advantage of being a definite, objective act—an act which not only expressed my return to religion, but ratified it and committed me to still further acts of expression.

I came out of the church feeling that nothing very much had happened. It was not till later that I knew my life was changed—as surely and as suddenly as if I had started up like a character in one of my own novels in the middle of a revivalist meeting with the shout: "Salvation's got me!" The world had turned upside down, or rather it would be more correct to say that I had turned right side up. Till then I might have been standing on my head—my highest faculties at the bottom, all that was inferior and restless at the top, and the whole thing very uncomfortable and ill-balanced. Now I felt at ease and had an entirely new and more useful view of the world. Moreover, I was free. I could breathe and move as I could never have done while I stood on my head. I was free and up-right and the whole wide world of God's religion lay before me. I had never before—and I don't think ever since—known quite such happiness.

3

I was happy. But I kept my happiness to myself. I told no one—I did not even let it overflow into my writing. I was now about half-way through the second version of *Tamarisk Town*, having picked up the discarded manuscript very shortly after fin-ishing *Little England*. In view of much that has been said of the bad effect of religion on writers in general and on me in particular, I cannot resist pointing out that I have done what most critics consider my best work after, not before, my return to it. *Green Apple Harvest* and *Joanna Godden* and the greater part of *Tamarisk Town* were the novels that immediately followed that event.

The fact is, of course, that judging by appearances, my first novel as an Anglo-Catholic is *The End of the House of Alard*, published in 1923. This is an Anglo-Catholic story and my position is obvious. The few who already knew could see it in *Joanna Godden* (which contains phrases and episodes which could have been written only by someone who was at least Catholic-minded). But the general run of critic and reader does not see those things until they are forcibly brought to his notice, and then—as I have found to my cost— he can see nothing else.

I do not think that there is anything in *Tamarisk Town* which would lead the reader to think that the author had "got religion" in the middle of it. There is, I confess, a very sharp division between the two halves of the book; but this has nothing to do with outside events (even with the troubles which made me put the manuscript aside for two years)—it is integral to the story. The fact that I had to let my heroine die half-way through the book was, as I knew at the time, a serious threat to its unity. I relied on Monypenny, the chief male character, and on the continuous background of the town itself to fill the gap and soften the edges. Unfortunately I found this feat quite beyond my literary powers, demanding as it did real technical skill combined with a fiery urge that should have swept the reader over the difficult place.

The break showed badly when *Tamarisk Town* was published in the autumn of 1919, and the critics were not slow to notice it. Frank Swinnerton called the book "a noble failure," but on the whole it was very well received. Only a few complained of my having left the country for the town; probably more would have done so had the novel been written later, but at that time I was not definitely labelled as a country novelist.

Reviewing had recovered all its pre-war energy; indeed it was advancing along new lines, for the "special" signed review outside the column was on the increase, while the column itself had in many instances discarded its anonymity. This was not, I think, on the whole, a change for the better, and the average review to-day is very much less candid and therefore less helpful than it used to be. I will not go so far as some in hinting of a literary racket —but it would be nice to be able to believe in one's reviews again, as I used to believe in the reviews of *The Tramping Methodist* and even of *Sussex Gorse*. I did not quite believe in the reviews of *Tamarisk Town*—already too many of my novelist friends were writing them. "Sheila, I had to say something against your book, or people would have been suspicious, knowing that I'm a friend of yours; so I said it was *dull. . . .*"

Tamarisk Town was the first of my novels to be published with Messrs. Cassel with whom I have remained ever since, that is nearly twenty years. It was also the first of my novels to sell more than a thousand copies. It sold three thousand to be precise, which though it sounds modest enough was nevertheless a marvellous multiplication. For eleven years I had counted my pounds in tens and my sales in hundreds; now at last I had the satisfaction of dealing in hundreds and in thousands.

Almost immediately I had finished *Tamarisk Town* I began to write *Green Apple Harvest*, using the name and the name only, of the novel Willy George had persuaded me to scrap five years earlier. I made a false start, and after I had written about ten thousand words I stopped and began again. My first conception of the story had been that the two brothers in it should have two contrasting kinds of religion. Bob Fuller, the elder, was to be as he ultimately was, the stormy sinner and revivalist; Clem Fuller, who in the published novel is a simple, charming soul with no more than a natural religion, was first conceived as a country Anglo-Catholic. The type exists, though it is more commonly female than male, and there is nothing incongruous in Anglo-Catholicism with Clem's character. But fortunately I saw my difficulties before I had gone too far. I realized that I should have to write the novel in two different moods—for one brother would be expressing me consciously and personally, and the other through that subconscious transmutation which was in those days my normal relationship to the people I created. I preferred the second method, so I decided to cut Clem's religion out.

It would be a great mistake, however, to think that I was entirely detached from Bob's religion.

CHAPTER FIVE

The last scene in which he is recalled from suicide by the voice of God speaking to him in the Sussex idiom expresses a belief which was fundamental to my religion then, as it is fundamental to it now.

"I am your God—döan't you know Me? Did you think I was away up in heaven, watching you from a gurt way off? Didn't you know that I've bin with you all the time?—that every time you looked out on the fields or into your kind brother's eyes or at your baby asleep in his bed you looked on Me? . . . Why wöan't you look and see how beautiful and homely and faithful and loving I am?"

This is not pantheism or nature worship; it is Catholicism—God in all things, no matter how simple and seemingly insufficient. It is the ground of the sacramental system, through which by the operation of the Holy Ghost nature gives birth to that which the whole world cannot contain.

Later on his brother says to the dying Bob:

"It sims unaccountable hard as you shud die in the middle of the month of May."

The answer comes:

"Reckon it sims hard. . . . But I've a feeling as if I go to the Lord God I'll only be going into

the middle of all that's alive. . . . If I'm wud
Him I can't never lose the month of May."

Actually it needs a poet rather than a novelist
to express the truth I was labouring with here. In
those days I was writing poetry too, though I did
not publish it till some time afterwards—trying to
express my sense of the union between the natural
and the supernatural which had come to me very
soon after my return to religion. One of the earliest
effects of this had been a very great heightening of
my natural and human susceptibilities. I know
nothing that carries more definitely than religion
the gift of "a sharper life and death." Looking back
on the days before one had it, one seems to have
been only half alive—joy clouded, sorrow evaded.
In those days too I had been aware of a certain
sense of limitation and frustration when I looked
on nature, as if she must always be withholding
something of herself from me. Now this sense of
frustration, of non-possession had disappeared, and
I saw a beauty in the Sussex fields that I seemed
hitherto only to have guessed at. The country of
Westfield and Brede and Udimore, Platnix and the
River Tillingham had been baptized into the same
reality as I. I wrote of this new creation, and my

verse was as genuine an expression of feeling as any I wrote under the compulsion of human love. Unfortunately I am not a poet—only someone who in certain crises finds prose inadequate.

4

Green Apple Harvest was published in the autumn of 1920, and was immediately successful. The reviews and the sales were so good that my publishers actually increased the advance on my next book, though they were bound by the contract to no more than a very modest figure. I have always thought that *Green Apple Harvest* is my best novel, and in this I have the support of no less an authority than George Moore. In fact, he liked the book so much that he urged me to re-write it, and I even started to do so under his personal supervision. We sat together in his dining-room in Ebury Street, *Green Apple Harvest* and *The Brook Kerith* on the table before us, and at the end of the first sitting had re-written the first three paragraphs. My departure for the country soon afterwards cut short the work—to my very great relief at the time, though I now feel that *Green Apple Harvest* re-written in the style of *The Brook*

Kerith would have been an interesting addition to the curiosities of literature.

My reasons for liking the book were not the same as George Moore's, and I confess that my opinion may be prejudiced by affection. The country scenes—the scenes of Bob Fuller's wanderings as a preacher, so reminiscent of and yet so different from those of *The Tramping Methodist*—are still dearer to me than any I have created, and the religion expresses my own deeper feelings more surely if less clearly than anything I have written since—in prose. Apart from my feelings, I think I have for once been successful in placing my characters in that middle light between realism and romance which is the best to read human nature by, and the story goes with a passionate swing which, if only I had been able to achieve it earlier, would have saved *Tamarisk Town*. The faults are my usual ones of enlargement—faults so closely bound up with my literary virtue that when at last I succeeded in getting rid of them, much of that went too.

Most of the reviews bore out my good opinion, but I had certain private critics who were not so flattering. Some literary friends told me bluntly that I was getting into a groove—I had already used the salvation *motif*, and as for Sussex, I had not only used it but worn it out. Religion must have had a softening effect on me, for I took this criticism to heart and proceeded to act upon it, planning for my next story a scene in the Channel Islands. I was still unable to think of characters without a background, and I do not belong to that school of writers which can create a background out of a very little knowledge, though I had shown myself willing to create one out of no knowledge at all. I knew and liked the Channel Islands better than any other part of the British Isles outside my own country (my Scottish obsession had died with my early 'teens) and I had with them also a connection of race and blood. I should quite probably have written a Channel Island novel if it had not been for W. L. George, who stepped in at this juncture and changed once more the course of my literary life.

"For heaven's sake, don't stop writing about Sussex just when you're beginning to be known as a Sussex novelist. The only way to success is to fit into a definite pigeon-hole in the public mind.

If you're always changing, they'll change too. You want to be labelled—then they won't forget you."

I listened to him, not with any definite intention of sacrificing originality to trade, but because I did not myself really want to change. Sussex had been from childhood so inextricably a part of my literary invention that to start afresh without it could be compared only to starting afresh as a soul without a body. I did not want to die that death.

I am not sure if I was right—if he was right, even from a business point of view. It is all very well to be labelled Sussex as long as the public wants Sussex; but if the public should take a fancy, say, to Samarkand, one is notably at a disadvantage. Even if one were to tear off one's label and stage one's next story in the heart of Samarkand, it would not do, as the public would still think one ought to be writing about Sussex. The label acquires a moral character after a while.

From the literary point of view, I am less inclined to regret my decision. Judging by tentative excursions made in other novels—to America in *The Challenge to Sirius*, to Sark in *The George and the Crown*, and to Yorkshire in *Iron and*

Smoke—I gather that I should not have written better if I had abandoned Sussex, and might very probably have written worse. The country-side of my childhood is, with all its limitations, a part of my literary equipment, and in giving it up I should lose a good deal more than a background. Also, paradoxically, a fixed background may in the long run make for more variety than a changing one. If our scenery is always more or less the same, we must at all costs vary our characters and our plot. It may be permissible to stage the same plot in London, Afghanistan, Hawaii and Timbuctoo, and many authors successfully do so; but those who stop in one place must have more than one story.

Up to this point I had been inclined to harp on one theme—the ambitious landowner; *Sussex Gorse* and *Tamarisk Town* were both studies in ambition, and so was my next novel *Joanna Godden*. If I had been able to shift my action to Provence or the Caucasus or Iceland, or even Northumberland or Inverness-shire, there is no saying how many times I might not have told this story. There are signs that certain of my readers would not have been displeased if I had done so over and over again; every one of my books has aroused some protest because it is not exactly the same as the last one. But though my literary conscience is not abnormally acute, there are some things it will not tolerate. Besides, I should find it boring.

5

Willy George was never merely negative in his advice. He did not discourage the pale, unsatisfactory novel I was writing when I first met him without giving me an idea for a very much better book; and now he did not urge me to give up the Channel Island notion without substituting a story which was very much more successful than that was ever likely to be.

The idea of *Joanna Godden* came to him suddenly, but not so impressively out of the void as the idea of *Sussex Gorse*. This time we were walking through a farmyard and he caught sight of a woman's name on a wagon in one of the barns.

"Why don't you write a book about a woman farmer?"

I objected that I did not like writing about women and had never before made a woman my central character.

[146]

"You ought to. It's time you wrote a novel about a woman. And you can do it—look at the woman in *Green Apple Harvest*. She must be a strong, ambitious, barbaric sort of woman, with a name like Hannah."

I pointed out that Hannah was the name of the woman in *Green Apple Harvest*.

"Yes, that's a pity; for it ought to be Hannah. You had a good name—Hannah Iden."

"Why not Joanna?"

"Joanna might do. And the surname should be something like Iden . . ."

I can't remember who first thought of Godden. For some time Joanna Godden was nothing but a name. I did not like the idea of writing about a woman. I felt I did not want to spend six months in female company. As a girl of eighteen, who knew scarcely a man besides her father, I had chosen a man for my central character, and had continued to do so ever since. Writing as I did, from imagination rather than observation, a man presented no more difficulties than a woman, and I definitely preferred a man's society. It was not now so much that I doubted my ability to write about Joanna Godden as that I did not want to. I thought she would bore me.

But though I did not jump at the idea as I had jumped at the idea of *Sussex Gorse*, Willy George was just as enthusiastic about it, and began immediately to work it out. He sent me, as before, some pages of jotted notes—and I began to see possibilities in the book. Joanna, with her reckless, splendid notions, her conceit and her warm heart, would not be such bad company after all. I decided to write her story, and directly I had started it, I found myself surprisingly at my ease. After all, though I had created men ever since the days of Adrian de Cæsar, behind Adrian himself lay Trimmer, first and female child of my imagination. It was not really more difficult to write about a woman than about a man, and I was glad I had been tempted to try it. As in the case of *Sussex Gorse*, I never discussed the book with Willy once it had been started, and also as in the case of *Sussex Gorse* he did not like it when it was finished. He said I had made Joanna too much of a virago.

Chapter Six

My heavy burden—In everlasting remembrance—Causes and effects of a return to consciousness—Author of a best
seller—Protesting too much—A marriageable clergy—Good-bye to Sussex.

I

Joanna Godden was published in the Autumn of
1921, and was received in a manner that made it at
first my biggest success and later my heaviest burden. Most authors find that sooner or later they
write a book which their readers never allow them
to forget. As far as I am concerned, *Joanna Godden* is that book. Though in many ways, I think,
inferior to *Green Apple Harvest* and even to *Little
England*, and in some ways inferior to *Sussex
Gorse* and *Tamarisk Town*, it did something to my

[149]

literary reputation which no earlier book was able to do in quite the same way. It was not a best seller, for it sold only about ten thousand copies which is about half the average best seller total, and actually less than a third of the sales of its successor, *The End of the House of Alard*. Its appeal was mainly to those with some share of the novelist's outlook—Joanna is essentially a "novelist's heroine" and since the days of *Adam Bede* it has always been easy to hit a certain section of the public with a little love child. I do not wish to appear ungrateful, but when one has written more than twenty novels it is sometimes trying to be known as the author of only one of them.

It is equally trying to hear *Joanna Godden* sighed over as the last novel I wrote before religion spoilt me as a novelist. The contrast between it and *The End of the House of Alard* is commonly put down to religion. I had taken to Anglo-Catholicism in the interval and according to the rather naïve views of authorship held by some readers and even by some critics, immediately sat down to write about it.

Actually *Joanna Godden* is full of clues to the author's religious position. Apart from the sympathetic portrait of Lawrence Trevor, the Anglican monk, there are several allusions to Catholic customs and ideas. Joanna's morality, too—her attitude towards divorce and illegitimacy—is definitely Catholic and Christian. Certainly the book's religion is more explicit, if less dominating, than in *Green Apple Harvest*, and would almost certainly have been recognized for what it was had *Joanna Godden* been published after instead of before *The End of the House of Alard*. As things were it aroused comment, and for fifteen years the novel has been held up to me as an example of the excellent work I used to do in the days before I became mixed up with religion.

From that point of view, perhaps, I was unwise to write *The End of the House of Alard*. When it first appeared a far-sighted friend said to me: "Now, whatever you may write for the rest of your life, you will always be suspected of religious propaganda." This I have found true; if Sussex is a label, religion is a dye and there is no getting rid of it. The public does not necessarily object to propaganda, but it likes the propaganda to propagate something it wants, like divorce, not something like Catholicism which it does not want and largely disapproves of. Criticism at once ceases to be candid, for the majority of critics so dislike the colour of one's thoughts that they refuse to look at any beauty there may be in the form that embodies it, whereas the minority whose view one is expressing can see no possible defect in that expression.

It is not altogether a useful state of affairs, for I doubt if a novel of propaganda ever converted anyone; as far as I can judge from my own experience, they preach mainly to the converted. I have sometimes wondered if religion should ever be made the subject of a novel—and yet how can one leave it out? In all save certain small groups who have sublimated their normal instincts in the gases of unending conversation, it exists as a powerful and universal force. It may be suppressed, inhibited or misdirected, after the manner of other instincts, but it is still there, colouring and directing human life for good or evil, according to whether it is or is not given healthy expression. To ignore it gives a very lop-sided view of the world. The number of people without religion in fiction is out of all proportion to the number in fact, just as is the number of women who die in childbirth. They

both represent a literary convention which is sometimes also mighty convenient, and one can always
say "it does happen," though the answer is "not so
often as all that."

Actually religion provides nearly as many good
situations as the sex-instinct—there are endless com-
binations, permutations, frustrations and deviations
which the novelist can use, and its effect on character (either by its growth or by its thwarting)
makes something new in the way of psychological
interest. I myself had used it many times before I
wrote *The End of the House of Alard*—in *The
Tramping Methodist*, in *Spell Land*, in *Isle of
Thorns*, in *Sussex Gorse*, in *Sirius*, in *Green Apple
Harvest*, in *Joanna Godden*; in fact I do not think
that there is a novel of mine where it does not
make some appearance—except *Tamarisk Town*, in
the middle of which I found it.

The difficulty about its appearance in *Alard* is
that it is professedly and obviously in a form in
which I myself believe. The sensational Methodism
or the conventional Anglicanism of the earlier
books could not possibly carry any propaganda
with them. Obviously I did not believe in these
things as I wrote them, or if I did my belief was

[153]

static and self-centred rather than dynamic and missionary. In *Alard* I was definitely challenging and proclaiming, and here—speaking from a religious as well as from an artistic point of view—my error lay.

I am not of course suggesting that an author should not write about what he personally believes, but that he should realize that to do so involves more dangers than to write about what he personally feels, since he is likely to find himself interfering in his own creation, destroying the balance of that transcendence and immanence which makes for an ordered literary cosmos. Actually I did realize this, but not so fully as I might, and I was too confident of my own power to overcome the difficulty. I did not grasp the fact which ought to have been obvious, that I had always been an imaginative rather than a reproductive writer, and that it was dangerous to start right away like this from a point well outside my imagination.

But looking back on that time, it is easy to see how I came to write the book. I had been an Anglo-Catholic four years, and I have already said that four years is the time it takes any external event in my life to be digested into literature. Also my attitude towards Anglo-Catholicism was less spontaneously religious than it had been at first; I was beginning to rationalize it, I wanted to proclaim it and justify it. This may mean that I was beginning to lose some of my faith in it, since it is a common idea that we rationalize and justify only that of which we are unsure. Or it may have meant simply that I was passing from poetry to prose— men often write poetry to their sweethearts but seldom to their wives; which does not necessarily mean that they love them less, but that poetry is not the language of security.

2

I did not, however, write *The End of the House of Alard* directly I had finished *Joanna Godden*. I began a book which was published later under the title of *The George and the Crown*. This was put aside, as *Tamarisk Town* had been, owing to a succession of personal troubles, culminating this time in the death of my father. I had never seen death before, but there was nothing that was terrible and very little that was distressing in this first encounter. On the contrary there was something altogether right and natural in my father, full of years and the love of his family and neighbours, dying quickly and painlessly of a disease incidental to old age. One could find no tears except for those left to mourn his loss. He went with dignity to the reward of those whose lives have never (so far as one can judge) departed from the ways of integrity and kindness. There are, as all Catholics know, souls even outside the visible unity of the Church who have never lost their Baptismal innocence, and I should not be surprised if my father was one of them. "The just shall be had in everlasting remembrance" . . . these words from the Mass for the Dead are his in a special manner. They come into my head every time I think of him. They appear in their Latin version on the flyleaf of the Missal which a Catholic patient who could never forget him gave to the little church that now stands in the fields he used to love. *In memoriam aeternam erit justus.* . . .

After his death I did not return to the manuscript of *The George and the Crown*; it had been put aside for a time that was both too long and too short for me to take it up again immediately—it would be easier to come back to it after I had written another book. The story of the Alards had been suggested to me by the news that the heiress of a certain large and important Sussex family had entered a convent. The idea came to me of writing the history of that family's last two generations as I had heard it from my father. It must be a more common history than I imagined, for the only local family that did not recognize itself in the book was the one I had in mind.

The religious interest was not, then, extraneous to my subject; it was the root from which the whole thing had started, and I was necessarily committed to it in some way. My failure did not lie in my inability to keep out an obsessive or incongruous idea, but rather in my treatment of that idea, which was not objective enough. I voiced it in dialogue rather than expressed it in action, and I did not sufficiently mix it with the other ingredients of my story—I was altogether too personal and exuberant. Up till then I had never gone to life for my novels, but now I had gone to it for much more than my "plot." For the first time I was writing from actual fact and experience—much of it my own. I was "in" this novel all through. Hence possibly its selling qualities, for artistic detachment does not as a rule make for big sales. *The End of the House of Alard* sold as no novel of mine has sold before or since.

The sales owed nothing to the reviews, which were nearly all unfavourable—some actually destructive. My friend's prophecy was being fulfilled, and I saw that my work was henceforth to be judged in the light of my critics' religious susceptibilities. I am not for a moment suggesting that *Alard* did not deserve at least a great deal of what it got; my objection is that the book's inferiority to its predecessors was almost universally put down to the religious element in it. Few critics who did not protest against this criticized it on other grounds.

Actually it is open to criticism in a number of ways. The swift and sudden collapse of the family may perhaps be paralleled in life—though I telescoped two generations to bring it about—but it is too hurried and forced as I have written it. There is also a fatal lack of inevitableness about the story, which should have swooped down on its ending instead of creaking to it mechanically at its author's obvious contrivance. But of these faults as well as of others it can be said that I have done worse things in earlier novels, and yet in each case managed to write a better book. The fundamental criticism which truly accounts for *Alard's* inferiority to, say, *Green Apple Harvest* or *Sussex Gorse*, was made by only one writer—the Rev. C. C. Martindale in the *Dublin Review*.

Writing of the South American scene in *Sirius* he states his belief "that she could similarly know almost anything, provided she had so soaked herself in it that she reacted as nearly as possible by instinct, and not consciously. . . . What, then, is the strange lack of comment in these books, such that when for once she does introduce her own appreciation she makes one jump? It certainly is not that she does not feel, but (can one say it without being rude?) she is far at her best, and wisely allows herself to be so, when she is not *thinking*. Take *The House of Alard*. To start with, the whole book is a thesis." . . . He then goes on to examine the weakness of that thesis, and the faults of observation and characterization by which I try to prove it. "These instances are accumulated to justify our surmise that in this novel Miss Kaye-Smith is not letting herself go to that uncanny second self in virtue of which she wrote her first admirable novels, and which was hardly a *thinking* self at all. . . . And this is a great pity. We can quite imagine that Miss Kaye-Smith thinks she *has* been more 'personal' in this last novel—that there is more of herself in it; well, yes, of that conscious self which was just what did *not* make the amazing success of her work so far."

This is, I think, the truth, and fully accounts for the difference between *Alard* and the earlier books; but I am not sure if the reviewer realized that the process he described was to a certain point inevitable—that a time was bound to come when I should no longer write from unconscious instinct but from conscious thought and observation. It is fatally easy to attribute any falling off in an author's work to some external event such as marriage or conversion to religion, losing sight of the fact that the deterioration may be equally due to inner changes of personality and consciousness. Of course external events may produce these changes, but equally such changes take place of themselves as one grows older. No one seems to look to the simple explanation of Anno Domini. Authors grow up, grow middle-aged, grow old. They pass out of their adolescent dreams, though perhaps they manage to retain them longer than most people, and enter on a new and adult relationship to life.

Now this, I think, is what had happened to me. Hitherto I had been, psychologically speaking, adolescent. I had spun *Joanna Godden* out of the same web of day-dream and fantasy that had made *The Tramping Methodist*. The later book is more definitely shaped by external knowledge and acquired literary skill—I did not write in a trance—but it is equally the work of that "uncanny second self" of which Father Martindale speaks, and which somehow when I came to write *Alard* had disappeared into the background, where it has remained ever since. There was no question of "not letting myself go to it." It just was not there.

This growing up process may have been hastened by religion, which often brings on psychological maturity by its unifying effect on the personality. Or it may have been brought about by the shock of my contact with fundamental realities in my father's death. Or it may simply have been due to the fact that I was now over thirty. I do not blame the subject of *Alard* for its onset. It is true that I had chosen an external happening in the world of facts, but there is no valid reason why my imagination should not ultimately have taken hold of this as it took hold of the stories of *Sussex Gorse* and *Joanna Godden*, both of which came from an outside source, or of the story of *Green Apple Harvest* which was based on the actual life of a preacher who at one time roamed the borders of Kent and Sussex with an eccentric gospel. The fact that I myself was consciously in the book may have hastened the withdrawal of my unconscious, but it cannot be solely responsible for it, or the next book to *Alard*, from which I was entirely detached, would have shown a return to the old position. Actually it did not. No book of mine since *Joanna Godden* has been written from that anteroom of consciousness which is in some of us so much more richly stored than consciousness itself. I sometimes fear that I shall never write so well with this new, unified personality as I did with a personality that was (shall we say?) a trifle split. In some authors to grow up may be an advantage, just as some people—most, in fact—are pleasanter as grown-ups than as children. But with others it is the contrary.

Apart from the effect of this new state of things on my writing—of which I was not at the time fully aware—I had no reason to regret what had happened. *The End of the House of Alard* might not be as good a novel as *Joanna Godden*, but it was infinitely more successful, and he must be a very saint and stylite among authors who does not prefer large sales and fat cheques to even the most eulogistic of reviews. I had written novels for eleven years without making more than sixty pounds out of any one of them, and often not as much as that. Then for three years things had improved and I had known the pride and pleasure—both since lost —of paying income-tax. Now I experienced the crowning though equally fleeting joy of being on the sur-tax roll.

Alard was a best seller both in England and America, ran successfully as a serial and brought in a number of commissions for articles and short stories. I had more money than I had ever had in my life—more than I knew what to do with, for I had no extravagant tastes and no prudent impulses to save up for the future. A certain amount of it went in clothes (I no longer had to rely on my nail-scissors and remnants of furniture cretonne), and a certain amount in travel; and for a time, till I learned better, I must have been the answer to every begging-letter-writer's prayer. But I have only a vague idea as to how the greater part of it went, for I kept no accounts. I was not used to money, and one of the chief joys of having it was not having to know how I spent it.

3

But the rewards of *Alard's* publication were not all material. The book made me known to a large number of Anglo-Catholics and gave me a new sort of fame among them. I met most of the leaders of the movement, and began to receive invitations to address meetings and congresses, which I was glad enough to do, as I was full of enthusiasm. At first Anglo-Catholicism had been primarily a religion to practise; but as my relation to it passed out of the initial, emotional stage into one more conscious, I saw it increasingly as a cause to be spread, as a movement to be advanced.

Up till now my religious position had been known only to a very small circle; to many it came as a surprise and not all were pleased. On the other hand, an author's name was not without its uses on notice-boards and hand-bills. The Anglo-Catholic party had just suffered a heavy loss in the secession to Rome of G. K. Chesterton. I cannot imagine that I filled his place any better mentally or spiritually than I should have done physically; nevertheless my appearance was opportune. Anglo-Catholicism did not boast many "names," that is to say names known outside ecclesiastical circles, and I soon found that they had plenty for me to do.

The expressed aim of the movement was nothing less than "the conversion of England through the Catholic Faith to the knowledge of our Lord Jesus Christ." To fulfil it the party looked neither to the Church to which it belonged nor to the Church which exclusively proclaimed itself Catholic. The former, it would say, had, while preserving at the Reformation the bare essentials of Catholicism, reduced herself to ineffectiveness; while the latter was a foreign intrusion—"the Romans," "the Italian Mission."

One had the sensation of belonging to neither. Technically, of course, one was a member of the Church of England, though one felt a trifle apologetic about it, and much more out of tune with its services and at variance with its official pronouncements than with those of the Church of Rome. For standards of doctrine and worship

Anglo-Catholics turned to what was officially called "the practise of the Undivided Church," but which was actually for most of us modern Roman custom. We always spoke reverently of the Orthodox Churches of the East, but we had not the patience or the leisure to imitate their age-old, age-long methods; nor did we altogether feel safe in the traditional atmosphere of Sarum, though the "English use" was more widely practised then than I gather it is now. The tendency was to approximate doctrine and ceremonial as closely as possible to those of Rome, though other ideas had their partisans and the ranks of Anglo-Catholicism were seldom free from controversy.

I should, however, be doing the party a grave injustice if I gave the impression that it was mainly ritualistic. It paid, no doubt, a disproportionate attention to externals, because external points were invariably those that received most publicity and opposition. Also, rightly or wrongly, Anglo-Catholics regarded them as connected in such a manner with fundamental ideas that to give up any one of them would be to give up something very much more important than, say, the wearing of vestments or the use of incense. But the main purpose

[166]

of the movement was to re-establish the Catholic *life* in England—the life of the Sacraments, the life of the Saints, that strong, merry life of freedom and discipline which they believed had once been lived in this country and could be lived there again by those who made the Incarnation of the Son of God the mainspring of their faith.

At that time I believed that the Anglo-Catholic movement was the divinely appointed way of England's return to Catholicism. Only in this respect were my beliefs and practices really different from what they are now. The change I made in 1929 when I joined the Church of Rome was mainly a change of allegiance, due to my conviction that Catholicism cannot exist apart from the Church which Christ himself established on the rock of Peter. Otherwise, there is no fundamental difference between what I believe and work for now and what I believed and worked for then.

My enthusiasm in those days blinded me to the movement's essential weakness, which was that it moved only in expressed defiance of an authority whose legitimacy was the very basis of its existence. The bishops of the Church of England were not only defied but even in some cases held up to the ridicule of their flocks, and the fact that they had by every "Roman" standard the right to forbid much that they forbade counted for nothing with these Anglo-Romanists. For this they had the excuse that if the movement had ever submitted to authority it would have come to an untimely end. From the days of Pusey onwards progress had been made only in defiance of the episcopate. But its later adherents had lost the distinction between a prohibition which is by Catholic standards heretical, such as the command of the Victorian bishops to their clergy to give up hearing confessions, and one which by those same standards is entirely legitimate, such as the forbidding of services other than those provided by the Book of Common Prayer. Looking back on those times, it seems as if we could have made our position much easier as well as fundamentally sounder if we had not exasperated the bishops with such trifles as the number of candles on the altar or the use of incense. But as I have already said, we had convinced ourselves that to give up any external meant the denial of "the doctrine underlying it," and many a clergyman would have held himself guilty of denying the Real Presence if he had had two candles on the altar instead of six.

Certainly a great deal of what we strove for was not worth the sacrifice we made to win it—the sacrifice not only of obedience to a proper authority but of the integrity of our own minds, which rationalized our position out of all logic and almost out of all sense. The final position of the movement seems to be in a sort of deadlock, for a number of its adherents have come to believe in the Infallibility of the Pope while rejecting his authority (in the matter of their orders and their personal responsibility for the ending of schism), treating him very much as all along they have treated their own bishops, a treatment which he is even less likely to find conciliating.

In my day we did not believe in the Infallibility of the Pope, though we—or at least some of us, for Anglo-Catholicism was never homogeneous—believed in the rest of the Catholic religion. At this time there was no question of my looking in the direction of Rome; I was boldly marching towards it. But the pathetic thing was that I had no idea of where I was going. If anyone had asked me I should probably have answered Catholic Canterbury, which, though I knew very well that it did not exist, I was determined should exist by the time I got there.

4

I did not think much—if at all—about the great Catholic Church on which my whole belief and practice was based. I had only one set of Catholic friends (who behaved throughout all this with admirable discretion), and I never attended Catholic churches, except when abroad (those in Switzerland I liked—they were so Anglican—those in Italy were a weltering nightmare). I regarded the Church of Rome as something intrusive and alien. It is our job, not yours, to convert this country, and every time you pray for the conversion of England we are the answer to your prayer.

The Catholic reaction to *Alard* had not been encouraging. Catholic critics had been annoyed by my blind eye deliberately turned on the Church, and one at least expressed himself almost viciously. On the other hand I know—for I have since been told—that a number of Catholics started then to pray for my conversion. To such it must have been a real disappointment when they heard I was to marry an Anglican parson. Indeed I can offer my marriage as an encouragement to anyone whose prayers seem to be in the way of being denied. On the surface, it meant the end of all hopes of me as a Catholic; for though I will not say that a parson's wife has never been converted to Catholicism, it is not a common event, and the odds against any unattached woman must be at least doubled by her marrying a clergyman.

Actually, however, my marriage was the very thing that brought me into the Church. Humanly speaking, I should never have entered it but for my experiences as a clergyman's wife and the close contact with the Church of England which they brought. Without them I should either have lived on as an Anglo-Catholic, hiding my head like an ostrich in the Catholic life of some "extreme" parish, or possibly, as had happened already twice before, I should have failed to maintain my contact with a purely subjective religion, and been left with an empty heart, now very much swept and garnished.

If my Catholic friends were disappointed, my High Anglican friends were more so—at least those of them that believed in the celibacy of the clergy.

[171]

This has always been a controversial point in Anglo-Catholic circles, and it is hard to see how it can be settled. On one side is the plain statement of the Book of Common Prayer that the clergy are free to marry, not as a concession to human weakness, but "as they shall judge the same to serve better to godliness"; on the other is the rule of a celibate clergy throughout the Latin Church. Supporting the Prayer Book is the custom of the Orthodox East, which enjoins a married clergy for its parishes, with the further argument that a married clergy is also the rule of those Eastern Churches in communion with Rome, so that Rome obviously does not see anything incongruous or unsuitable in uniting the Sacraments of Order and Matrimony. Supporting the celibates, however, is the fact that these Eastern rites, whether Uniat or Orthodox, insist that marriage shall take place before ordination—that no form of episcopacy except the Church of England tolerates the idea of a *marriageable* priesthood.

I did not have to change my views on this subject in order to be married, for I had always believed that the pro-celibacy party was in an impossible position. Whatever the Anglo-Catholics did or said their clergy would still be marriageable, and to behave as if they were not savoured perilously of make-believe. Their marriageableness was proclaimed by the fact that they were constantly getting married, and many of the leaders of the movement were married men, though the tendency was to assume that their fall had taken place in bad old "moderate" days, before they knew any better. I hope I am not being unnecessarily brutal if I suggest that such popularity (and it is not very great) that a celibate ministry enjoys among the laity of the Church of England is due to the very fact that it *is* marriageable—that if it were, for instance, in the same position as the Roman priesthood, it would not have even the support it has. The tradition of a married clergy is very firmly established in this country, though from a clerical point of view there is a great deal to be said in favour of an unmarried staff, especially in town churches. The Rector of the church where my prospective husband worked would not employ a married curate, so he had to resign his curacy, and we decided to make our future home in London.

It was the first time that I had the prospect of living in London for more than a few months, and though I did not mind leaving the town of Hastings itself, I sometimes wondered how homesick I should find myself for the country outside it. How should I manage to write far away from the fields which were not so much a background to my novels as the soil from which they grew? I already knew London well enough to feel pretty sure that I should never be able to use it as a literary setting, and I could not imagine myself writing a novel in which the place was not at least as important as the people. As for any other part of England, it was vain to think that I should ever come to know it as well as I knew the country of the Kent and Sussex borders, for my knowledge of this was based on the first perceptions of childhood, and for more than thirty years it had been a part of everything that counted most in my life. . . . My books, of which it was more than a part, my friendships and love-affairs, which were also memories of roads and trees and marshes, my religion which had been unable to clothe itself either in prose or verse without the mirror of this same country-side, of its months in whose changes heavenly wisdom is reflected as in a glass, of its fields where the saints must walk before I can see them clearly.

[174]

CHAPTER SIX

I am not a regional novelist for any reason but necessity. I have never deliberately chosen or marked out any part of Britain as my own preserve, and I write about Kent and Sussex (West Kent and East Sussex) because I am as much their child as any character in my novels. I felt at home in that country even after I had left it, and my imagination fled there for a number of books—*Saints in Sussex, Joanna Godden Married, Iron and Smoke, The Village Doctor, Shepherds in Sackcloth*, which were all actually written in London. Inspired by home-sickness and half a life's memory, these books are not, I think, topographically less vivid or less true than those I wrote actually on the spot. As novels they have their drawbacks and deficiencies—these grew on me while I was in London—but as pictures of the country-side they are, I should say, at least equal to their predecessors and definitely ahead of their immediate successors. I wrote them much in the same mood as that little girl of six, who, shut away by

the ugly houses, guarded by city red

still dreamed of Platnix Farm.

Chapter Seven

Clergymen's wives—I attempt the impossible and discover a national neurosis—
North and South Kensington—Fumblings
and failures—The Ultramarines—I find
that I belong to the Church of England.

I

THE break with Sussex was more complete even
than I had expected, for my mother was taken ill
the day before my wedding and died shortly afterwards. As my sister had died in the first months
of the same year, this meant the end of my St.
Leonards home. It was not there even for a visit.

But I now had my own home. I was fortunate in
that the two sides of my life had slightly overlapped,
whereas they might have gaped. I cannot pretend
that my mother's death meant the same to me as it

[176]

would have meant had it happened before my marriage—apart from the fact that, like my father, she went full of the benediction of years to the further joy of meeting him. My sister's death, because it happened unexpectedly, because she was young and because I had to struggle to her bed-side through the nightmare of a railway strike, affected me very much more deeply.

I have not written much about her here. Her very early self appears in my two semi-autobiographical tales of childhood. Later on, ill-health combined with an adventurous spirit changed her into a very different creature from the stolid, cheerful Moira of *The Children's Summer* and *Selina is Older*. It is remarkable that, brought up identically as we were, under the same strict nursery laws, we should have developed into two such different people. Though very good friends, we grew up utterly unlike each other in tastes, temperaments, ideas and abilities. Let those take notice who regard a child's mind as a blank slate on which life and education may write what they please.

I was now a clergyman's wife, and some of my friends shook their heads, imagining that I would forsake novel-writing for Mothers' Meetings, Sunday Schools and Clothing Clubs. It was somehow taken for granted that I should share my husband's work in a way no one would have expected for a moment had he belonged to any other profession. There are, of course, clergymen's wives who are no less than unpaid curates, but such are as a rule either qualified for the post in their own persons (as teachers, nurses or social workers), or else they live in lonely country parishes where their status is much the same as that of colonial wives. My husband was curate at a church in Notting Dale, and though on the main question of to marry or not to marry the Anglo-Catholic party does not speak with a united voice, on a secondary point it is unanimous, and that is, that once a person marries, his wife must keep out of the way. I found myself in a little group of clergymen's wives who were as the lilies of the field in so far as parochial matters were concerned, though in their own homes many of them did the work of nurse, teacher, housemaid and cook.

I am inclined to think that the clergyman's wife is in some ways the most maligned woman of the community. In novels she is nearly always represented as stupid, domineering, interfering, a gossip,

a busybody and uncharitable—always uncharitable. Lack of charity is the most common accusa-
tion brought against people who are supposed to
be religious—it may be because it is the fault that
stands out most glaringly against the background
of the Gospel. My own experience of the clergyman's wife is that she is very far from deserving
any of this. Both the London parishes in which
my husband worked were singularly free from
gossip, meddling or social tyranny, and in each
case I think the vicar's wife may take the credit.
In country parishes, also, I have found the parson's
wife the first to help and protect the poor girl
who "gets into trouble"—contrary to one of the
most respectable traditions of British fiction, which
always puts the first stone in her hand.

As a clergyman's wife I had as much time for
writing as I had had as an unmarried woman; though
this would not have been so if we had had to depend
on the exiguous salary on which the Church of England expects its married curates to live like gentlemen. In that case I should have had to scrub and
cook like so many of my co-wives, and I know of
nothing more destructive to the literary impulse
than scrubbing and cooking. I did not, however,

[179]

immediately start another novel—my mind was a little restless after all that had happened and preferred to deal with the commissions for articles and short stories which had been accumulating since my marriage. Besides, I had just had a novel published.

The George and the Crown appeared in the early spring of 1925. It was in some ways a new venture, for a large part of the action takes place in Sark. But though the Channel Islands were the only part of the world for which I could ever at one time imagine myself leaving Sussex, this experiment showed me clearly that I could write of them only from the outside, from the visitor's aspect. Even my mother's blood was not able to let me see their people through their own eyes. The book was well reviewed and sold well, but it seemed to fall singularly flat. It is not, I think, among the worst of my novels, but I have very little affection for it. Perhaps this is because of all that happened while I was writing it—between the first page and the last I lost and gained so much that the novel itself seems only a background to the sharpness of my own life. Certain critics expressed their satisfaction that I had given up writing religious propaganda; but their

[180]

relief was short-lived, for my next book was called uncompromisingly *Anglo-Catholicism*.

Strangely enough, I wrote it at the suggestion of W. L. George, who was now allied with the publishing firm of Chapman & Hall. I cannot put it on the same level as his suggestions for *Sussex Gorse* and *Joanna Godden*, for *Anglo-Catholicism* is not the sort of book that could ever be particularly useful or welcome. Any monograph on this form of religion has to be controversial on two sides, it is on the defensive when dealing with either side of its hyphen—Canterbury or Rome. It also has a number of internal controversies to settle, and many Anglo-Catholics found my book too "extreme." The non-religious reviewers hated it, and my religious label was tied so closely round my neck that it nearly throttled me.

It certainly impaired the circulation of the book that immediately followed. *Saints in Sussex* is partly the re-issue of the verses I wrote when I first returned to religion (which were published in a limited edition by Messrs. Elkin Matthews); it also contains two newly written mystery plays. If I were to be allowed to choose which work of mine I should like to be remembered by, I should choose

[181]

those two plays—*if* (and it is a qualification that disqualifies) they could be as I had intended them, as I had seen them in that happy land where unborn books live before they come to earth to be spoiled by their authors. To stage the Gospel stories of the Nativity and the Passion in the country-side of my youth and love had been for several years my supreme literary ambition. I carried it out on the emotion of nostalgia for the land I had left, and I was not big enough for the task—I could never have been big enough if I had waited all my life. Can anyone, even on the impulse of emotion, recover that medieval simplicity which saw both the manger and the cross in its own fields? I doubt if it can be done, but certainly with me the effort was spontaneous. It was no literary gesture.

The critics thought it something worse—a religious gesture. Whether they would have done so but for the publication of *Anglo-Catholicism* I cannot tell. But I was accused of having brought two incongruous elements together in the interests of propaganda. Whatever I did—or more notably failed to do—it was not this. There is nothing incongruous between Sussex and Catholicism (is not every country place in England soaked through with Catholic tradition?) or even between Sussex and Anglo-Catholicism (is it not the Brighton and South Coast religion?), and the book does not contain a vestige of propaganda, unless quotations from ancient liturgies are such of themselves. It has plenty of faults, but the faults were in me, not in my subject; and it was my subject that was generally attacked.

In the course of nearly twenty years' experience I have come to the conclusion that in England we are not quite normal on the subject of religion. This is not surprising if you apply to the general public those psychological theories which are with monotonous frequency applied to the individual, and if you accept the hypothesis that religion is a fundamental human instinct, the supression of which may be attended by quite as many disastrous consequences as the suppression of any other.

Four hundred years ago the Catholic religion was forcibly suppressed in this country. Without the slightest attempt to change or educate public opinion it was entirely swept away. The system established in its place bore so little resemblance to it in the popular mind that it was looked upon as a game, until fines, imprisonment, torture and death

[183]

for those who refused to play it established it in
sober earnest. Is it to be wondered that so gigantic
an inhibition should create an equally gigantic neurosis? The attitude of many people to-day towards
Catholicism, in fact towards any kind of religion,
is not unlike that of an inhibited type of spinster towards sex. They giggle nervously or become angry
and excited if it creeps into the conversation, while
the "poison pen," sure sign of psychological de-
rangement, is never so active as when brought out
against those who have publicly identified themselves with it in any way.

Anglo-Catholicism rouses almost as much opposition as the real thing, one of the reasons being, I
think, that anyone who has not actually been an
Anglo-Catholic believes that they are in bad faith.
Even now, long after I have left them, I find myself
continually defending their good faith against those
who think it incredible. The attempt to lead a Catholic life in the Church of England seems so illogical
and outrageous that they cannot believe it is sincere.
But this does not account for the whole opposition,
for people often take other people's bad faith quite
calmly. It is probably another aspect of that same
anti-Catholic neurosis. The trouble with Anglo-

Catholicism is that up till recently anyone who belonged to the Church of England felt himself safe
from Rome; but now the Church of England itself
has betrayed him and the hated, inhibited idea rises
out of the Protestant security of her forms and cere-
monies. It is like finding that the mad dog has followed you into the house.

2

I was disappointed with the reception of *Saints in
Sussex*, a book specially close to my heart, and one
which I had not expected to stir up so much opposition. Actually my interest in controversy was dying down. It had persisted for some time after my
marriage, and not only in my books, for I had ad-
dressed congresses in Northampton, Leicester,
Bournemouth and London. But now I was beginning to feel that one can have too much of this side
of religion and also to realize that my vocation lay
elsewhere. I was not a first-class speaker, and it did
not seem worth while leaving my home and my
literary work just to appear on handbills and plat-
forms. I felt that it was time the Anglo-Catholics
collected another author—it seemed to be always
the same old circus travelling round.

I had now been in London for over a year, watching the workings of Anglo-Catholicism in conditions very different from those in which I had seen it before my marriage. I had an affection for the little church in Notting Dale where my husband worked—it was almost lovably hideous, and had a cosy, simple atmosphere that appealed to me more than the magnificence of the better known Anglo-Catholic churches. But whereas these were always full of devout worshippers, this poor little place was always nearly empty. Out of a parish of ten thousand, the normal Sunday morning congregation was between eighty and a hundred. It stood in a district that had once been fashionable, but had now sunk into a mixture of shabby gentility and positive squalor. In the good old days there had been two churches in the parish—a large one, which now stood deserted and empty, except for occasional use as a parish room, and the small one which was nevertheless too large for its congregation. The population had not decreased—on the contrary, what had once been the imposing residences of single families, were now crowded tenements, swarming with souls, most of whom were nominal members of Ecclesia Anglicana, but scarcely any of whom ever availed themselves of her ministry—except for baptisms and churchings, which were said to have a high therapeutic value.

Anglo-Catholics have done some fine work in the slums both here and in other parts of London. The names of St. Alban's, Holborn, St. Peter's, London Docks and St. Mary's, Somer's Town, are not only the names of star churches of the movement but of centres of devoted service and social reform. But in the case of these and similar churches there is a great deal of outside support, either from school and college missions or from well-to-do people living in other districts. Our little church had no such outside support, and did not seem able to manage without it. Anglo-Catholicism alone was not enough. Incidentally we were not always quite sure what that was, or rather in what manner it should be expressed, and there was sometimes rather an unpleasant atmosphere of controversy among the few who did come to church.

My husband and I both grew anxious and depressed. We were used to crowds and enthusiasm and people falling over one another to work and pray. We told ourselves that Poor Jimmy (as we called the house of God) was a failure, though in our hearts was an uneasy feeling that he was more representative than we would allow. After all, no one could have worked harder than the Vicar and his curates. The Romans, we said loftily, do nothing for their people; and we never looked inside their churches to see if they were full or not.

We were both very much relieved when my husband was offered a curacy at one of the leading Anglo-Catholic churches, this time in South Kensington. Once more we should find ourselves back in the familiar atmosphere of crowds and enthusiasm, working for "the faith." We felt that nothing could be done to revive Poor Jimmy, and we were right; for not long after our departure the Vicar also left and the Bishop put in an incumbent who worked on totally different lines, so that much of the little we were able to do was undone.

We were sorry, however, to leave North for South Kensington—to exchange the flaring contrasts of wealth and poverty for an atmosphere of uncontrasted and mediocre prosperity. The district of Notting Hill and Notting Dale has always seemed to me the most interesting in London. Chesterton has sung the praises of the Hill, but the Dale has been dismissed as mere slumdom from most literary imaginations. It is true that there are slums—but what slums! The slums of East London are a desert of sordid monotony—they seem to have been designed for slums and built for the deliberate purpose of segregating the more unsightly part of the population. Rows of small, squalid houses go on and on for ever till the eye gets used to them and vision itself becomes mean. In Notting Dale the slums come up impudently to the back doors of mansions. Turn out of Holland Park Avenue into Princes Road and you are in a different land—the street lamps are fewer and gutters are strewn with rubbish, as befits those who do not pay mansion rates. But the mansions themselves are still there, though clothes-lines hang from window to window, and women sit suckling their children at the top of long flights of steps between marble porticoes. There is no humble dropping of the roof-line, for these houses were built for rich men in the days when it was considered good to be just four miles from the city, a pleasant carriage drive. Even the square gardens are still there, with tangled bushes and grass like hay.

The people, too, are quite different from the average East End slum population. Here there is very little real Cockney. The inhabitants are many of them the second generation of country folk, who seem to have congregated here—perhaps because many of the houses have little gardens where flowers and vegetables can still be grown. There is also a good sprinkling of gypsies, renegade and housebound, but expressing their eternal love of roving in their trade, which is nearly always "pushing something round on a barrer"—oranges, tortoises, draught-stoppers, ferns or flowers, according to the season.

It is the only part of London that has ever given me a literary inspiration—with humiliating results. I made it the setting of a long-short story called *A Wedding Morn*, whose fortunes clearly proclaimed that I must never do such a thing again. It was commissioned by a well-known magazine, but when the editor saw it, he promptly sent it back—he could not possibly publish a London story under my name; it had not even occurred to him that I would not write about Sussex. As it was a commission he had to pay for it, and an amiable adjustment of our interests was made, by which I agreed to pass on to him whatever I received for it elsewhere.

But his fee had been exceptionally large and no other magazine could offer it, so he lost quite a good sum by the transaction. It is the only time I have been given money to go and sing in the next street.

A Wedding Morn was written too late to be included in *Joanna Godden Married and Other Stories*, which appeared in the spring of 1927. I had never felt easy as a short story writer, and of the few I had written still fewer seemed to me worth collecting. But half the book is taken up by the title story, which attempts to wind up the fortunes of Joanna Godden. The novel itself had ended on such an uncertain note that several readers had written to ask for a sequel. Some were obliging enough to tell me exactly what form it should take; one of them, I remember, was so determined that Joanna's son should go to Eton that he suggested—as this would be difficult to manage in the case of illegitimate offspring—that the novel's final catastrophe should turn out to have been a "false alarm," leaving Joanna free to make an advantageous marriage and produce the Etonian respectably.

I did not feel equal to writing another novel about Joanna—my novels are dead selves which, as a rule, I have small inclination to revive. But the idea of a story of thirty thousand words appealed to me; it is an agreeable length from the writer's point of view, and by this time I too was interested in Joanna's fate, having heard so much about it from other people. Unfortunately I found it impossible to think of her still as she had been in the novel. I imagined that she would, as a mother, have lost much of her bravura—mothers do—and have become a quieter woman, which was not what my readers wanted. They wanted her to be the same undaunted Joanna—the same as if suffering and loss and humiliation had never touched her. The critics more reasonably objected that the continuation of her story is flat and thin in comparison with its lustier beginnings. I was not, I am afraid, so interested in her as I had been in the earlier book, as I ought to have been if I was to write a sequel. But I gave her, I think, a husband who would have suited her admirably—the very man she ought to have married.

Three years had passed since the publication of *The George and the Crown*, and it was perhaps natural that some people should think that London was not suiting me as a novelist. Three years does not seem an alarming interval, but all my best-known novels had followed one another fairly quickly, and my publishers were beginning to think it time I produced another. They were pleased when I told them I had started a full-length novel. The idea of *Iron and Smoke* had been with me for some time, but I had become interested in my other work and might have been satisfied to go on indefinitely experimenting with it had I not been discouraged enough.

Iron and Smoke was not a very good novel. It suffered from the same trouble as *The End of the House of Alard*—the trouble of my "thinking." What in early days I used to feel had been fresh and vital, but what I now thought had oft been thought before. This time the book's deficiencies could not be put down to the initial drawback of a religious thesis—they were plainly in myself and in my method of writing. My novels were becoming external—rationalized. I made an effort to go back to the old intuitive methods in *The Village Doctor*, published a year later; but it was not a success, being altogether too slight and conventional a story.

The critics and public were not slow to discover

the failings of these two books—neither my reviews nor my sales were what they once had been. Opinions varied as to the causes of the decline—London, religion, my marriage were all blamed, though none exactly met the situation. A decided falling off of literary invention had shown itself in novels written before my marriage and coming to London, while religion coincided with *Tamarisk Town* and my most highly praised work.

The actual source of the trouble was less easy to remedy than any of these would have been, since it lay deep in changes of my own growth and consciousness—changes which were in themselves normal and good, but which from the literary point of view had robbed me of a valuable quality. The disappointing thing about them was that when they first set in they had seemed, in spite of their effect on the artistic side of production, to improve at least my chances of a popular success. But now even this compensation was lost. And I could not go back—I could not write again in the old way, any more than I could be twenty-five again.

3

I was not actually aware of all this at the time—it came with later experiment and reflection. But of course I realized that my expectations of these last two books had not been fulfilled. I do not mean that I had flopped in any decisive way—my sales were still what many novelists would envy and my reviews were unenthusiastic rather than unkind. But I had definitely failed to realize my own high hopes for myself—hopes that had filled me in the days when I wrote *Sussex Gorse* and *The Challenge to Sirius* and which ought to have been fulfilled by now.

None of this hurt me, however, as much as it would have hurt me ten years ago. In those earlier years my only contact with real happiness had been through literary success, but now I touched it at two other points—my marriage and my religion. The former had turned out a complete success, though when I married I had been far too good a novelist to imagine that it could—hence, perhaps, one reason why it did. The latter continued to satisfy my deepest desires, though it was not on the surface in quite so good a case, being covered with ecclesiastical irritations.

The change from North to South Kensington had not been so satisfactory as my husband and I had hoped. It is true that we had found all that at one time we thought we most wanted—a fine

church, a crowded congregation, magnificent services, and "the full faith." But somehow none of these
things seemed so good now that we had them as
when we had them not. The balance was now on
the other side, there was too much worship and
magnificence, devotion was exhausted by surfeit,
the eye and ear were being worked unceasingly
without rest. The soul felt squeezed out of it all.
One longed for something quiet and simple and
above all uncontroversial.

For controversy had followed us across London,
and now took an even more disedifying form than
a squabbling congregation. The congregation here
was united under a popular vicar and his still more
popular wife, but it was united against all that
should have led and supported it outside. We were
in a constant state of warfare with the rest of the
Church of England, especially the official part. In
Notting Dale we had obeyed the Bishop's rulings,
in South Kensington we defied them. The Bishop
of London could never be called a persecuting
prelate, and Anglo-Catholics have more freedom
in London than in any other diocese, but there
were some things he would not tolerate. One was
the service of Benediction and the use of the Mon-

strance, and the strange thing is that our Vicar felt bound to obey him in the first instance and equally bound to disobey him in the second. We did not have Benediction, but we had a service called Adoration, which the Bishop had licensed, and at it we used the Monstrance. The congregation was not blessed with it as at Benediction; it merely stood on the altar as a symbol of defiance.

Those were the days when the New Prayer Book was fighting its stormy way through ecclesiastical politics, and it was thought that its chances with the House of Commons would be materially increased if those bishops who were not considered too good at disciplining their clergy should make some sort of gesture to show what they could do in the way of enforcing its regulations should it ever become law. The Bishop of London made a special appeal to those clergy who had gone beyond his very wide concessions, urging them to return to the rules he had made for "extra-liturgical services" and give up the use of the Monstrance. Many of them fell into line, but some stood out, among them our Vicar, with whom the Monstrance had become a matter of conscience—it was, he said, Our Lord's own appointed way for showing himself to his people. The Romans, I remember thinking, would scarcely go as far as that.

We were now living and working with the most extreme type of Anglo-Catholic, known to their detractors within the Movement as the Ultra-marines. The Infallibility of the Pope had not yet become common doctrine amongst us, but we were on the way to it. In more than one church, Mass was said in Latin, processions of the Blessed Sacrament were held on the feast of Corpus Christi, and certain of the clergy recited the Breviary offices in addition to those of the Book of Common Prayer. We were not a large group, but we represented the spearhead of the Movement and held that what we thought to-day the rest would think to-morrow.

I was not entirely at my ease among them. Some of their practices seemed to me downright silly. It seemed silly to think that by reciting Indulgenced prayers we could gain the Indulgences promulgated by a Church which regarded us as heretics and schismatics. It seemed silly to follow the Lenten rules of the Cardinal Archbishop of Westminster instead of those of the Bishop of London. But much more disquieting from a Catholic point of view was the attitude of the group towards authority in general. It seemed to think that the bishops had no right to control their dioceses, even such bishops who had again and again shown their sympathy with the Catholic movement. I was told it was my duty to attend the services they had forbidden, and to support the clergy who were defying them. If I argued the point, I was reminded that every Catholic practice had at one time or other been forbidden by the bishops, and that only by defiance had the Movement moved at all, which was perfectly true.

This being the case, what exactly was the Anglo-Catholic view of a bishop's authority? If he had not the right to regulate worship and discipline in his own diocese, what rights had he at all? The solution appeared to be the same as that which Father Ronald Knox found existing shortly before his conversion—to regard the bishop simply as a machine for ordaining and confirming, the hereditary dispenser of a totally mechanical grace. Even in those days this appeared to me a rather horrid superstition; but it was difficult to think of any other theory that would justify both our attitude towards the Church of England and on remaining in it.

Though not quite at ease among the extreme Anglo-Catholics, I should have felt uneasier still on the more moderate side of the Movement, the side that was definitely Anglican in its aims and atmosphere. The Church of England had never been much more than a name to me. From the moment I had passed out of the unformulated religion of my childhood, the only religion I had wanted had been the Catholic religion—first seen dimly as "High Church" and then more definitely in Anglo-Catholicism. I had always believed that as an English woman I should be able to find and practise that religion within the Church of England; my education and environment had shut out the Church of Rome except as an ultimate disloyalty. But apart from the Catholicism which might be found in it, the Church of England had no attraction for me and very little meaning. That being so, it is not surprising that once having associated myself with Anglo-Catholicism I should find no ties to hold me to the Anglican shore, but should drift out with some other very insecure craft on that Ultramarine ocean whose farther shore is Rome.

Quite a number never reach that shore. Some float round until they come back and remain safely

Anglican for the rest of their lives; some anchor off
the windy coasts of "modernism" and find freedom in the winds and waves that buffet them to
pieces; some find queer little coves of their own
and live sheltered there; some sail right up to the
Grand Harbour, but being unable to negotiate its
narrow entrance sail away again.

Up till now, though more than once I had gazed
towards that not so distant harbour, I had always
regarded such a look as frailty. There could be no
entry save as a fleet—to seek it alone would be
treachery and cowardice. Like nearly all Anglo-
Catholics, I looked towards an ultimate reunion
of at least a part of the Church of England with
Rome, though I put that event even further into the
future than many of my co-religionists. To make
an individual "submission" would simply be running away from the battle that would end in an
honourable peace. Whenever the thought came to
me I pushed it aside as a temptation due to disillusion and weariness.

My husband, I knew, sometimes had that temptation too, and treated it in the same way. Like myself, he had no strong feeling for the Church of
England as such. He had gone straight from Quak-

erism into Anglo-Catholicism, and had very little
experience of ordinary Anglican ways. As a clergyman, however, he was more closely involved with
official Anglicanism than I could possibly be, and
his conscience was troubled by conflicting alle-
giances. He was not so terribly light-hearted about
the Anglican episcopate as certain Anglo-Catholics
were inclined to be. After all, it was the only authority that he had accepted at his ordination. A
vague, overriding authority, such as that of "the
undivided Church," whatever that was, did not
seem a clear enough revelation to justify the breaking of promises. And yet the authority he had accepted was, he felt convinced, ineffective, time-
serving and vitiated with heresy.

The controversies round the Revised Prayer
Book filled him with disgust and disappointment.
The bishops had offered so much in their speeches,
but seemed afraid to see their promises in print.
He had at one time looked forward to this new
Prayer Book as to a rule that he could accept,
which would set his conscience at ease both with
the Church of England and with "the undivided
Church." But the whole labour of official Anglican-
ism seemed to be to show him that these two au-

thorities were incompatible. The Church of England appeared afraid to proclaim itself openly and irrevocably as Catholic—in this respect the new Prayer Book was no better than the old.

He had little sympathy with the official talk of "comprehension," feeling that there could be no logical comprehension of opposites. The candidates and converts whom he instructed in the Catholic faith ran the risk, on leaving him, of being taught the very opposite. He had joined the Church of England, believing her to be the Catholic Church in this country, but he found that Catholicism was at the best only tolerated and at the worst openly contradicted.

I did not, of course, have to deal with this aspect of the situation, and had I been alone it might not have troubled me. After all, I had not joined the Movement in quest of an authority, but in quest of a religion; as long as I was allowed to practise what I believed to be the Catholic religion I did not much care what the bishops thought or did. My husband, however, having been brought up as a Quaker, with no authority save that of the Inner Light of the Soul, had expected on leaving Quakerism to find an external authority to supersede it. But apparently he had still to follow the directions of the Inner Light, as he had nothing else to tell him when to obey and when to disobey the External Authority.

We discussed these problems together, but the solutions we suggested to each other were none of them the solution we ultimately found. We had the Church of Rome at the back of our minds; but, apart from the question of loyalty, we did not feel that it offered a satisfactory way out of our difficulties. In common with most Anglo-Catholics, we knew little or nothing about it. We attended its services when we were abroad, but never in our own country, and our constant discussions and criticisms of it were based largely on fallacies.

For us the Holy Catholic and Roman Church in England was rather a sinister corporation, and our attitude towards the Romans, as we unfailingly called them, was a mixture of uneasiness, admiration, suspicion and contempt. We told ourselves that their numbers were exiguous and that their influence was nil, except with the Vatican, where they were always successful in checking any beginnings of goodwill towards Anglo-Catholics. The parish priests took very little trouble about their flocks and were quite indifferent to the large number of lapsed among them. The atmosphere of the whole thing was foreign—congregations being composed mainly of Irish, while worship was conducted in a manner that could be pleasing only to Neapolitans. Learning and enlightenment were firmly discouraged, and the whole thing was over-organized —a "rigid uniformity" without variety, elasticity, freedom or humour.

Convinced as we were of all this, it is difficult to see how the Church of Rome could ever have been a temptation to us. And yet, believe me that it was. The very uniformity that we affected to despise had a secret appeal for us as we rocked in the midst of chaos; the obscurantism that we deplored seemed on the whole more wholesome for Christ's flock than the half-baked modernism distributed weekly among the uninstructed from Anglican pulpits. We resisted such thoughts as snares—it was our business to stay where we were and bring order (not uniformity) out of chaos, an enlightened (not obscurantist) Catholicism out of modernism. We were English, and the Church of England was the Catholic Church in this country. Until the day of corporate reunion it was our duty to remain in her and do what we could for her; temptations to do otherwise were only attacks of "Roman fever," such as every Anglo-Catholic is liable to at intervals.

Nevertheless at this time I noticed that my attitude towards the Church of Rome was changing in rather a curious manner. Though I disapproved of her methods and regarded her as being in a false position in this country, I found myself with growing frequency taking her part against those who attacked her. I reproached myself again and again for this championship, accusing myself of disloyalty; and yet whenever there was another attack, up again came my defence. Moreover, I could not help seeing that it was based on nothing less substantial or more reprehensible than a love of justice and sober fact; if I examined it afterwards, I never found anything to withdraw, anything wrong with what I had said except that it was I who had said it.

4

I had once been told that an infallible cure for Roman fever is to visit Southern Europe. I had already seen and disliked the Church on the northern shores of the Mediterranean, so I had high hopes of restoration to normal religious health when, in the September of 1928, my husband and I set off on a cruise to Sicily. Here we might reasonably expect to find the Church at its most repulsive and return home thanking heaven we were not Roman Catholics. But the remedy did not work.

We arrived in Palermo and visited the cathedral, hoping to be appalled. We were full of anticipations of dirt, neglect, slackness and superstition, and it was really a shock when even the first of these failed to materialize and we found the cathedral both well swept and well kept. It was, moreover, full of the population of the city, hearing Mass impartially according to the Latin or the Greek rite, being baptized, getting married, saying its prayers, talking, resting or walking about. It was, in fact, a spiritual version of the streets of Palermo.

We found it impossible to keep comparisons with Anglican cathedrals out of our minds. These certainly are not a spiritual version of the cities in which they stand, but something select and apart, museums rather than market-places; frequented chiefly by tourists, except for rare intervals when religion comes in and the tourists go out. In the cathedral at Palermo there were certainly tourists, but they were few in comparison with the people

[207]

of the place, for whom it provided a cheerful, lively, democratic, spiritual home. There were treasures to be viewed, but they were a side-issue to the religion which it was obviously the main business of the cathedral to dispense. There was garlic and there were fleas, and the Mass was as much a homely scramble as it had been in Northern Italy. But this time one could not blind oneself to the fact that this place was really providing religion, and providing it not only for the pious few, but for the many, for the workers, for that man in the street to whom Anglicanism gives such a raw deal.

Later on that same evening, as I watched the huge baroque mountains of Sicily disappear in the clouds beyond the western sea, I felt that I was leaving behind me a living, working, democratic faith—leaving it for one that was mincing, cold, limited and psychologically unreal. The next day was Sunday, and a clergyman on board would celebrate Holy Communion for a few ultra-good passengers, amongst whom my husband and I would self-consciously find ourselves. No one would have thought us ultra-good had we approached the altar at Palermo—it was there for everyone, good and bad, who happened to be in grace, part of a working, everyday religion. But we could never have approached that altar, we were debarred from it, cut off by something more separating than the sea—schismatics . . . the altar to which we had access was in the ship's lounge, and that cold, exclusive Church of England service—from which nine-tenths of the ship's passengers and all the crew would stop away—was our own deliberately chosen substitute for the breadth and homeliness of the Mass. It was all very well at home to dress ourselves up and pretend that things were different. Here, cut off from Anglo-Catholicism, we knew where we really belonged.

Chapter Eight

The second half of a conversion—The serial of the saints—A handsome farewell present?—Dropping the hyphen—The Huguenot farm—The parting of friends.

I

A CERTAIN Anglican divine when asked by a Methodist if he had been converted, replied:

"Yes, many times; and I hope to be as many more."

I cannot claim to have been converted more than twice (three times, perhaps, if you count that childish adventure in the church at Throwleigh), and I am not sure if these two conversions are not really two parts of the same experience. Certainly the first would have been unreal and incomplete without the second and the second would have been impossible without the first. All that I did and learned as a High Anglican, far from being denied by my joining the Catholic Church, was given a new meaning and validity; while if I had turned to the Church without first having turned to religion my Catholicism would have been nothing but an empty form.

With many people—with most, I imagine—these two processes are simultaneous. They come into the Church because they want religion. I might have done this if I had been less impulsive and sentimental eleven years earlier. But I had allowed myself too easily to be repelled by externals and I had shrunk from the greater difficulties involved by joining the Church of Rome; with the result that I found I had still to face them. I was like a patient who has tried to stave off a major operation with a minor one and then finds that after all he has the major operation to undergo.

Not that I have any right to talk of major and minor in this connection. In many ways my return to religion in the Church of England was a bigger event than my changing from the Church of England to the Church of Rome. It was not so sensational, but it was more fundamental, since all I changed in the latter case was an outlook and an allegiance. Beliefs, practices, ideas and aspirations were very much as they were before.

I might say perhaps that my first conversion was of the heart and the second of the mind; or that they were the emotional and intellectual halves of what ought to have been a single experience. Certainly intellect had very little to do with my first turning to religion. My soul was hungry and took the food it wanted without asking more than a few perfunctory questions. The vital questions came later, and my turning from the Church of England to the Church of Rome was the answer given them by reason and experience.

When I say that the second part of my conversion was a conversion of the mind, I do not mean that it was mainly the result of thought and study, or of a minute survey of the Anglican position. It was rather the effect of my reason, of my normal human powers of observation and deduction, guiding my opinion on religious matters as they guided it more or less in secular affairs.

Even after what I had seen in Palermo Cathedral I did not want to be a Catholic in the sense that I had once wanted to be a High Anglican. Rome had no romantic attraction for me, no glamour; I

was merely impressed by her efficiency and spirit-
uality in the very place I had expected to find
her at her most degraded. I was driven back half
resentfully to the conclusion that I had expressed
in *The Challenge to Sirius*—some ten years before I
actually made it—the conclusion that Romanism at
its worst is better than the best in Anglicanism. Its
superiority, too, I saw as essentially spiritual, and
the appeal it made was to that wider Catholicity
which concerns not only dogma but sex, class and
temperament, a democracy of the spirit.

Another lesson I had learned at Palermo was
that I belonged to the Church of England. This
may seem incredible to those with no experience
of the Anglo-Catholic mind, of that curious rationalizing process by which thousands of English
Christians range themselves in opposition to the
Church with which they are factually in communion. Many of them see so little of its official
workings and take part only in services that are so
alien to its spirit that it is possible for them to maintain this delusion indefinitely. They drug themselves with the assertion that the Church of England is the Catholic Church in this country and
dissociate themselves from its more sinister work-

ings on the Continent. My husband and I hardly ever attended Anglican services when we were abroad, and if we had actually been staying in Palermo we should have gone to High Mass on Sunday with all the satisfaction of Catholic worshippers. It was being on a cruise, with our Sundays under Anglican auspices, that gave our outlook for the first time a touch of realism.

On our return, however, we did not actually contemplate "going over to Rome." We still regarded the Catholic Church's appeal as a temptation, even though that appeal was now less to a love of order and orthodoxy than to a more spiritual idea of what a Church should be. But we were definitely shaken, and not in a good position to face the assaults that were soon to come upon us from the Anglican side.

That winter the Revised Prayer Book, still further revised, was thrown out for the second time by the House of Commons, to the bitter humiliation of all who looked to Canterbury for light and leading. The Ultramarines were rejoiced to be spared the legal enforcement of a rite which they considered even worse than the old one, for the very reason that it *could* be enforced. But only a few of them can have failed to realize the very hard blow which the temporal power had dealt the spiritual. It looked as if chaos and bewilderment must henceforth be more than ever the lot of the Established Church.

In the smaller world of our own parish, too, things were not going too well. The Vicar had decided to resign, and as a change of vicars nearly always involves a change of curates, my husband found himself obliged to think of another job. Here at once a fresh difficulty arose, for he now felt that he could not again make to his Bishop those solemn promises of obedience which his conscience would not allow him to fufil. Moreover, if he were appointed to a living—and he had had the offer of one in Oxfordshire—he would have to read out and publicly declare his adherence to the Thirty-nine Articles, most of which he regarded as heretical.

Of course we could neither of us help seeing the impossibility of such a situation, though we never discussed it except in its immediate, material aspects. My husband once said that the time might come when it would be impossible for him to remain in the Church of England except as a layman. But in that case, surely, I thought, it would be impossible to remain in it at all. An army in which one can fight conscientiously only as a private, without personal responsibility for the cause in hand, has no claim on any man's duty or sacrifice.

Yet I could see my husband's point of view in wishing to remain in some capacity an Anglican. His position was different from mine. A change for him would be much more drastic and fundamental than it could ever be for me, for it would mean the abandonment of his priesthood. The Catholic Church has condemned Anglican orders as null and void, and has from the earliest times made it her practice to re-ordain those clergymen coming to her from the Church of England; if my husband "went over" he would automatically cease to be regarded as a priest. Moreover, being a married man, he could not be ordained in the Catholic Church, and the change from clerical to lay life might well be more devastating than the change from Canterbury to Rome.

I could not imagine myself joining the Church without him, but I would make no attempt to influence anyone who had so much more to sacrifice than I had. I became convinced that any decisive move must be made by him and not by me. I was not yet in a position when it would be impossible for me to continue as an Anglican, though I was extremely uncomfortable and sometimes extremely unhappy.

2

For the Catholic Church had once again made an overwhelming spiritual appeal. This time she did it through the life of St. Teresa of Lisieux, whose canonization had just taken place, only thirty years after her death.

It is difficult to describe the impression this young saint made on me. It was not only the beauty of her life, the charm, wit and sweetness of her recorded words, or the lovely simplicities of her Little Way. It was rather the realization of that sanctity, that heroic virtue, that sublime love being offered to the modern world. Here was a saint who if she had been alive to-day would scarcely have been old—a saint of our times, showing the world that the *Acta Sanctorum* is no closed book, no worn papyrus of the Early Church or illuminated tome of the Middle Ages, but an up-to-date serial, illustrated with photographs. The holiness of little Thérèse linked itself with the vigorous life of Palermo Cathedral as part of the great natural, supernatural, ancient, ever new appeal of Rome. Nowhere else but in Rome, I knew, could either this vigour or this holiness be found.

In the Church of England one is given the impression that sanctity as well as miracles came to an end with the Early Church. The Anglican Kalendar is astonishingly poor and bare; it was drastically cleared at the Reformation and no name has since been added to it (with the doubtful and disputed exception of King Charles I) till the Revised Prayer Book cautiously inserted a few commemorations, the latest of which is five hundred years old.

I shall naturally be told that Sanctity is not an affair of the Kalendar, and if the Church of England has no official saints later than the twelfth century, it does not follow that she fails to encourage or to recognize holiness, but merely that she does not record and publish it. To which one simply retorts: Why not? Presumably a Church's greatest glory is her holiness, and her holiness is the holiness of her members. It seems strange that she should ignore and suppress her achievements in the only field where success is really worth while. One cannot imagine a country that should ignore its great men, its heroes, its poets, its philosophers and scientists. If one were inconceivably to hear of such a country, one would conclude either that it had no great men, or, worse still, that it was indifferent to their merits.

I was disturbed by the holiness of Rome—or rather, I should say, by the fact that I was cut off from it. This surely was the heart and blackness of schism. I was cut off from the Altar of the Saints— of St. Teresa of Lisieux, of St. Teresa of Avila, of St. John of the Cross, of St. John Vianney, and all the rest of that great cloud of witnesses—just as I was cut off from the altar of the people—the people of Palermo, Preston, Peking, every part of the world where the Catholic Church draws together all classes, colours and races. I was cut off, not by any personal conviction but because I belonged to a Church which had deliberately cut itself off four hundred years ago. It seemed useless to try and comfort myself with the thought that if I had been alive then I would not have subscribed to the Act of Separation. The point was that I was subscribing to it now.

It was in the refusal of this comfort alone that my position differed from that of many of my fellow Ultramarines. Most of them acknowledged themselves in schism, but held that they were not responsible for an act committed some hundreds of years before they were born. Their business now was to bring that schism to an end by working for what they called Corporate Reunion with the Holy See—that is, the reunion of the Church of England, or at least the Anglo-Catholic part of it, with the Church of Rome on the same basis as certain Eastern Churches which have been admitted by Rome as Uniats. This hope seemed to me even then to be founded on an unreality—the conception that the case of the Church of England is in any way parallel with that of those Eastern Churches, which are historically as old as Rome and had established their traditions, customs and liturgies long before the schism which cut them off. It seemed quite useless to compare these Churches with the Church of England, whose separate liturgy, customs and discipline originated with her separation from Rome and indeed in protest against Rome. There was also the further question of Anglican orders. The orders of these Oriental Churches were unimpeachable, and nothing more was required than for their priests to accept the jurisdiction of the Holy See. But Anglican orders have always been held by Rome to be invalid, and it seemed vain to hope, as my co-religionists confidently hoped, that the Church would ever reverse or even modify this attitude, ratified so late as 1896 by a formal pronouncement of Pope Leo XIII.

Neither in regard to the past nor to the future could I accept the hopes and rationalizations of my fellow Anglo-Catholics. I knew myself to be cut off from the source of life and holiness in the Holy Catholic Church. I felt myself to be guilty of that schism in so far as I remained in it after I became aware of it, and I did not believe that there could be any end to that schism save that taken by the individual on his own responsibility.

3

All this time I was writing a novel called *Shepherds in Sackcloth*, the last novel I wrote completely as an Anglican. When it was published, an Anglican paper remarked that it seemed impossible that it should have been written by anyone who contemplated, however remotely, leaving the Church of England. This shows the difference in a point of view, for to me the book is the story of a growing disillusion. An Anglican may not, perhaps, be unduly depressed by the tale of a clergyman whose ministry is at almost every point opposed and thwarted by his own bishop; but to a Catholic it strikes chill. Actually I had planned the book in much the same spirit as I had planned *The End of the House of Alard*, but it came to be written very differently. The original story-scheme is followed, but works out mainly as a character study, which was my secondary purpose.

I may thank my growing disillusion with Anglo-Catholicism for making *Shepherds in Sackcloth* a better story than it might have been. It is not so good a novel as *Green Apple Harvest* or *Joanna Godden*, but I think it is better than anything I had written since; and it has more tenderness in it than any other novel of mine except, perhaps, *Little England*. I really loved the old parson and his wife, and, as actually written, there is no propaganda in their story beyond the desire to make them better understood.

CHAPTER EIGHT

The clergy has suffered in novels from the fact that fiction is not usually written nowadays by men and women who know much about clerical life. Jane Austen and Trollope were so very literally at home in it that they can be allowed an occasional caricature—Mr. Collins and Mrs. Proudie are the legitimate and well-earned fun of writers who have shown us in a dozen ways that they know what they are writing about. But the clergymen of modern novelists are nearly all caricatures. They seem either to be a perverted company of sadists and sex maniacs, or else they are revoltingly smug. The author never seems able to imagine them as ordinary people, with normal thoughts and affections, leading for the most part prosaically normal lives.

"What on earth do they *talk* about?" a certain literary woman asked a friend who had just been staying at our house, and she seemed surprised when she got the answer, "Just what other couples talk about." She had apparently expected that a clergyman and his wife would talk of nothing else but Church and parish and religion. It is true that the clergyman's job may incline him, like any other job, to talk more shop than outsiders find entertaining, but of all the number I have known—and it is quite a large one—I have never met one who conformed either in speech or manners to the rules of his cloth in modern fiction—still less in his fundamental attitude to the reality behind his job.

In writing of old Mr. and Mrs. Bennet in *Shepherds in Sackcloth* I was writing objectively of what I knew. I was still without the help of that intuition which had written my earlier novels, but then neither was I rationalizing a thesis. If I had ever had a thesis I had discarded it for a picture, and I think that my picture, unlike my thesis, has the advantage of being true. Ecclesiastically the book was not the "handsome farewell present" the Anglican newspaper called it; but from another standpoint it was all that and more. I had lost my faith in the system, but not my affection and admiration for those who were still struggling to work it. I am glad that my last novel as an Anglican should have been a tribute to two of the worthiest and the most misunderstood members of the community—the English clergyman and his wife.

4

Should I ever have joined the Church without my husband? The question is as unprofitable as its

CHAPTER EIGHT

companion—would my husband ever have joined the Church without me? Both questions are unprofitable because they did not arise. When in both of us our convictions reached a point at which they could no longer be hidden, we found that they were exactly the same. Neither of us had to reason or persuade; all we asked of each other was explanation and suggestion.

Our silence on the main subject of our thoughts had also been kept for the same reason. At first we had been afraid of "upsetting" each other; but after a time that honesty which must be a part of marriage compelled us both to reveal what we were thinking. And lo and behold! we were thinking the same. Our minds had worked on parallel lines, which had met at last in defiance of mathematics.

He spoke first, releasing me from the bargain I had made with myself, and the first question that I asked him was the first that any Anglo-Catholic would have asked:

"What about giving up your Orders?"

The answer he gave was what any Catholic would have given:

"That goes in with the rest. If one accepts the Church, everything else follows."

[225]

He had grasped the point that I had missed till then—the point that the question of Orders comes after, not before, the question of authority. Once we had accepted the idea of an infallible Church we were bound in logic to accept her ruling on the minor point of Anglican Orders. My difficulty had been that in my approach to Rome I had reached infallibility last of all. Once again, in this second conversion, the cart had come before the horse.

This return to lay life was, speaking externally, the biggest change Catholicism would make for him and, through him, for me. Apart from this there would be very little alteration in our religious habits, for we were not changing a creed, but an allegiance. Looking back at those months, I can still say that I have never changed my religion. My mind has developed certain ideas, but these developments have never involved any change of direction, and religion, if it is anything, is a direction, the compulsion of the whole life along a certain way. At one time both my husband and I thought that, ecclesiastically speaking, we had reached our journey's end. It was true that another city lay beyond, but that was a city of foreigners—not for Englishmen. It was only when we entered it that we knew we were at last in our own country—our native land.

Our entry was made easier than it is for many. We had, as it were, already been through a long period of instruction; we were familiar with the doctrines and practices of Catholicism—we had not to learn these from the beginning, or from near the beginning, as so many have had to learn them. The water-pots were already full of water; all that was needed was for the water to be changed into wine.

We had an easy time, too, in other ways. For one thing, we were financially independent and therefore were spared the squalid anxiety which is the price most convert clergy and their wives have to pay for the truth. We were fortunate, also, in being able to give up our place in the parish without a fuss, as part of a normal parochial change. Nearly six months elapsed between our leaving South Kensington and our reception into the Church, so that we were spared the stress and scandal which sometimes attend those clergy who for one reason or another are unable to be properly off with the old love before they are on with the new.

Most of all, we were lucky in having a new work waiting for us. My husband did not have to go through that period of unplaced inactivity which is such a trial to the convert parson, even when he can afford to endure it. The work came to him through an idea he had formed as a sort of compromise at the beginning of his uneasiness about the Church of England. He had thought of giving up regular clerical duty and settling near some country church that would be glad to avail itself of his services—thus avoiding the difficulties attached to an Episcopal license. The neighbour-hood of Brede in Sussex not unnaturally occurred to us. It had been the ecclesiastical magnet of my girlhood's days and still maintained the traditions of rural Anglo-Catholicism, after the manner of the church at Vinehall in *The End of the House of Alard*, though it was not quite such an obvious wish-fulfilment as that dream. Naturally my whole heart opened at the thought of going back to the country which I had seen only in occasional teasing glimpses since I left it five years ago. We looked at the oast-barn at Hayes Farm, with a view to turning it into a house. But it was not suitable for various reasons; and my husband's wish to be even of occasional use in the Church of England had become so overlaid with difficulties that we had given up all thought of it when the offer of another farm in the neighbourhood unexpectedly came along.

Little Doucegrove, a farm which plays an important part in my early novel *Spell Land*, is one of the many in this corner of Sussex which owes its origin to French settlers entering the country as Huguenot refugees. Robert Douce, a native of Beauface, was woodcutter and miner to Sir William Sidney at the furnace of Panningridge, near Salehurst, and was granted letters of denization in 1544, in the name of Douce or Dows. Doucegrove, in the heart of the Sussex iron country, may well have been a settlement of his descendants. The first half of the name is pronounced Dows, and the second is probably an eighteenth-century embellishment (the place on one ancient map appears as Holmgrove, and until quite recently was sometimes known as Petty Doo), for it certainly does not date back far enough to be a corruption of the Saxon gryfja, for pit (as in Skinningrove), though there is a field close to the house still known as the Pit Field.

When my husband and I went to see it we were

[229]

on the edge of Rome, and the neighbouring Anglo-Catholic Church meant nothing to us. Our objections to the place came from the Roman side—it was too far from a Catholic church, nine miles from the nearest. Would it be right for us to settle so far from the Mass? We were still enough Anglo-Catholics to be unable to imagine religion without frequent church-going.

Yet we bought it, in spite of its isolation; and almost immediately afterwards found it was our business to provide for the religious needs of the scattered Catholics of the district. First in a stable loft, then in a small church built in a neighbouring field, a congregation varying from less than a dozen to more than fifty has assembled Sunday by Sunday. Yet when we first took the place we had no idea that there was a single Catholic in the neighbourhood. It was a work that quite definitely seemed given us to do; we should never have thought of choosing it, or even—in those early days—have guessed that it could be chosen. As for many years there was no resident priest, it meant more "parish work" than I, certainly, have ever done in my life. To visit the sick, round up the backsliders, teach the children, care for the sanctuary, take the collections, "answer the Mass," are all of them things I should never have dreamed of doing in either of my husband's parishes. Indeed, I have never felt more of a clergyman's wife than since I ceased to be one.

5

Our first plan had been to go to Rome for our reception into the Church. We thought this a course that would give a minimum of shock and offence to our Anglican friends. Unfortunately Rome would not be practicable till the autumn, and summer had barely come. We saw ahead of us some difficult months between two worlds.

We spent a part of the time in France and a part in Sussex near our future home. Little Doucegrove was a ruin standing in a wilderness—broken walls, broken floors, broken roofs in the midst of tangled orchards and neglected fields—so there was plenty for us to do. I also corrected the proofs of *Shepherds in Sackcloth* and started its successor *Susan Spray*.

This too had a religious idea, but one so remote from my present experiences—being inspired by the recent visit to England of a notorious American

[231]

evangelist—that I had no doubt of being able to write of it with all the detachment necessary to prevent its being reviewed as propaganda. Unfortunately it appeared too soon after my conversion for some critics to believe me without design. The *News Chronicle* spoke of "Jesuitical propaganda" and "the novel of propaganda" was the heading of the *Manchester Guardian's* review. Both reviewers imagined *Susan Spray* to be an exposure of the evils of Protestantism and an attack on women preachers, though I can truthfully say that I had intended neither. I had been taken with a character, and had transposed that character to a period which interested me and to the only country-side where I felt at home. Incidentally the book was the most successful I had written since *Alard* and recovered for me much of the ground I had lost with the critics and public.

It had been planned entirely during my Anglican days, but most of it was actually written after my reception into the Church. This did not, after all, take place in Rome. As the weeks passed at Northiam, my husband and I found that we could not wait so long as it would take us to travel to Rome in October or November and then go through a course of instruction. Our Anglicanism was gradually shredding off us. When we first made our decision we had gone on with Anglican practices for a while, though we found in them an increasing unreality. But we were reaching a point when this would become impossible. Anglo-Catholicism had already done so. Strangely enough it had lost its meaning before the rest of the Church of England.

It seemed useless and senseless to struggle to maintain an outward conformity after any sort of quickening spirit was gone. Neither tact nor courtesy could ask all that of us. We changed our plans. We would go to Rome after, not before, we had become Romanists, and the first thing to do was to find some priest to instruct us. My husband wrote to a Catholic friend who, he thought, might know of one.

"I don't mind who it is," he said, "as long as it's not a Jesuit."

"Nor do I—as long as it's not a Jesuit," said the last of Anglicanism in me.

Why we both objected so much to Jesuits I am not now sure. Anyhow heaven did not take our objection seriously, for it was a Jesuit who in-

structed and received us. My husband's friend
wrote in reply to his letter that Father Martindale
was at Rye, eight miles from us, and he had ven-
tured to tell him of our decision; would we go
and see him there?—mentioning the house of my
one set of Catholic friends.

So in the house where Father Martindale had
first read *The Challenge to Sirius* he gave us our
first instruction in the Holy Catholic and Roman
religion. We had a few days earlier made our last
communion in the Church of England, in all the
simplest, slackest circumstances of moderate Anglicanism. No incense, no vestments, no crowds
marked *Ecclesia Anglicana's* last ministrations to
her departing children. We saw her last as herself,
and I shall never forget her last words to me.

"For in Christ Jesus neither circumcision avail-
eth anything nor uncircumcision, but a new creature. And as many as walk according to this rule,
peace be upon them and mercy, and upon the
Israel of God. From henceforth let no man trouble
me; for I bear in my body the marks of the Lord
Jesus. Brethren, the grace of our Lord Jesus Christ
be with your spirit. Amen."

These words read to me and to five or six others

that village Sunday seemed as I heard them words of farewell—mine to *Ecclesia Anglicana* as well as hers to me. "Neither circumcision nor uncircumcision, but a new creature . . . peace and mercy . . . the marks of the Lord Jesus . . . Brethren, the grace of Our Lord be with your spirit." I like to think that thus, mystically at the Altar, we parted friends.

Epilogue at Little Doucegrove

CONVERSIONS to Rome are not unlike marriages in a certain type of fiction. The interest is concentrated on the events leading up to them and then the protagonists disappear. They go off in a cloud of bridal tulle or ecclesiastical incense and are no more seen. The presumption is that "they lived happily ever afterwards." But the public is cynical nowadays, and knows that neither marriage nor conversion is really the end of the story.

Among Anglo-Catholics there is a firm belief that those who join the Church of Rome lose soon afterwards either their religion or their wits. I have had the satisfaction of rescuing two eminently sane people from the mental homes where High Church rumour had placed them, and not long ago an unknown Catholic wrote asking me for some information about myself, as she was worried by the insistence of her Anglican friends that since "going over" I had lost my religion entirely.

Actually the parallel between Catholicism and marriage is a fairly close one. The convert does not

[236]

necessarily live happily ever afterwards, any more than the bride and bridegroom; but it is his own fault, and not the fault of the system, if he does not live a very much fuller, richer and better life than he lived before. He will find in Catholicism as in marriage a stabilizing effect, also a more adult, objective attitude towards life, which for that very reason becomes in the eyes of the world less romantic and less exciting. Dreams are no longer necessary for happiness, and poetry has ceased to be explicit in words, but is, rather, implicit in things. Just as the evidence of a happy marriage does not lie in the couple's exclamation of rapture or the embraces they give each other—especially in public—so in a happy Catholicism there are fewer shouts of joy, more acts of penitence, less outward bustle and protestation, more turning away of the soul to her own quiet home. That is why most converts have so little to say about themselves after joining the Church. Their history is like the history of a happily married pair—not half so interesting as if it had not been half so happy.

In my own case I can guess one reason why certain Anglo-Catholics believe that I have lost interest in religion—apart from the unconscious wish to prove that all conversions to Rome are disastrous. I now no longer take any public part in religious affairs, and they have forgotten that I ceased to do so some time before I left the Church of England. I had grown tired of finding myself always in the same little group of speakers. I knew that I had an importance which I did not deserve and which I should not have had in a larger community; for I have not the gift of effective speech, and what I have to say could be—and now is—more impressively said by others. My work as a Catholic lies in another, more obscure direction.

By almost everyone outside the Church, Catholics are regarded as untiring proselytizers. This, of course, is true of many, and naturally the proselytizers, whether clerical or lay, working in missions or over the tea-table, are better known to non-Catholics than those who have no special tendencies or abilities in this way. In a sense it is true that no good Catholic would want to keep his faith to himself, but there are many loyal sons and daughters of the Church who feel no special urge to carry their message into the highways and hedges or even into the houses of their friends. I personally am not good at making converts, for I dislike using persuasion as much as most people dislike using force; but ever since coming into the Church I have for one reason or another found it my business to help in the feeding of those sheep who are already in Peter's flock, but inclined to wander for lack of pasture. I sometimes feel honoured and amazed that I who stayed outside the fold for so long and so much of my own choice, should have found this work waiting for me to do almost from the moment of crossing the threshold.

When I was an Anglican we talked a great deal about "the Roman leakage," and now I am a Catholic we talk about the same thing, but in a way that makes me feel that we were not in the first place quite sure what we were talking about. For one thing I knew nothing of the actual figures. The number of Catholics in England has been estimated (roughly, for in this case it is impossible to get the figure exact) at about four million, while the number of Easter Communicants stands at between two and a half and three million—that is about the same number as the Anglican Church produces out of a total that can scarcely amount to less than twenty million. If from the Catholic Church there is a leakage, from the Church of England there is a flood. It must also be remembered that the majority of Catholics find themselves on leaving school in a society which is definitely non-Catholic. Neither their religious ideals nor their moral standards are those of the world around them; they may also find themselves cut off by distance or by the nature of their work from a Catholic church and a Catholic priest. The number of those who fall away is, therefore, really less surprising than the number who manage to keep true to their religion in the face of so many difficulties.

Another mistake I made as an Anglican was to believe that the Church has no concern for those who fall away from her, concentrating all her energies on making converts. In this I was gravely wrong, for the English hierarchy is well aware of a problem which they regard as crucial and with which they are grappling in a number of ways. The Southwark Travelling Mission is one diocese's effort to deal with the situation. A car equipped with all the apparatus of religion travels round the country districts of Surrey, Kent and Sussex, and each Sunday Mass is said in some outlying spot where there is neither church nor priest.

It was the Southwark Travelling Mission which

started the oratory at Little Doucegrove, visiting it every three months for a period during which so many Catholics were discovered that it became necessary to have Mass said monthly and then weekly. In four years the numbers had increased to a point that required a resident priest, and the oratory was amalgamated with a similar one at Tenterden. A year later both these oratories were found impossibly small for their growing congregations, and the loft at Doucegrove and the ballroom at Tenterden were abandoned simultaneously for newly built churches.

When I lived in this neighborhood as an Anglican I was not aware, apart from the towns, of the existence of any Catholics at all. Indeed, for a time before my reception into the Church, I went through a certain stress, feeling that by my act I was separating myself from the people and the soil I loved.

I need not have troubled myself, for I am not farther from the people of the fields as a Catholic than I was as a member of the Church of England. Sussex is not a "religious" county in the sense that Cornwall and Sutherland are "religious," and if there is any local or typical religion it is the religion

[241]

of the Chapels, where the people's language is spoken and their ideas prevail; or else it is the religion of the labouring man who on a Sunday evening leans over a gate and gazing down at the earth feels more than he can think. With both these forms of religion I have more in common now than I had before.

Nevertheless, I was surprised to find Catholics, country-bred Catholics, Sussex Catholics, living near me at Little Doucegrove. I had been told that I should find them, but I did not believe it, and it was almost a shock to have our little oratory so crowded at its first Mass. Most of the congregation lived at from seven to ten miles from their parish churches at Rye, Battle, or Goudhurst—enormous rural parishes that meet in the fields round Little Doucegrove—and as they were working people, some of them even without bicycles, the problem of Sunday Mass must until then have been a serious one.

Who are these children of the dispersion, living either by choice or by accident remote from the means of grace? The answer comes at once even to the tongues of Catholics: exiled Irish. But as a fact there are seldom any Irish among us here.

One or two Dutch farmers have settled in the district, but for the most part we are all plain English, converts or the children of converts. Moreover, as the neighbourhood is purely agricultural, we have very few exiles from the industrial north. Some of us have names that Sussex has known for centuries.

Jack Harman (his real name is as typically Sussex as the one I have chosen for his disguise) found himself by some strange accident in a Catholic church at the time of Vespers. He was so pleased with the service that he continued, with the help of a convenient 'bus, to attend every Sunday. This attendance, according to local theory, made a Catholic of him right off. Morning service is not of so much account as evening service in the country, especially among farm people whose hours it does not suit at all. When Harman was a Wesleyan he never went through any ceremony of reception or initiation, nor did he ever attend Holy Communion which he regarded as a service for the ultra-saintly, or any other kind of morning service; and yet he had considered himself a good Wesleyan. For several years he attended evening service in the Catholic church, thinking himself as good a Catholic as any there.

His conversion had always been a puzzle to me till I heard his story. How anything so slow, so inarticulate could have gone through the psychological upheaval involved by a change of faith and custom was a mystery, solved by the discovery that there had been no upheaval at all, but a change as slow and natural as the growth of a tree. After a devout attendance of many years, he came to realize that Vespers to the Catholic is not quite the same as Evening service to the Wesleyan, nor are Mass and Holy Communion "for good people only." He was already at heart so good a Catholic that the step further was of little cost. He took it as he might have stepped across the lane.

The establishment of a regular Mass every Sunday has since diluted our original congregation of working people with families of the "retired" stamp. But nowadays it is not only the professional classes that can earn retirement before old age, and a number of workers retire into the country, helping out their savings with money made by rearing chickens or taking in lodgers. Some of these are Catholics, and the presence of a church influences their choice of a spot to end their days in—though I have been startled by the number who take for granted that there are Catholic churches everywhere and buy a house without any preliminary inquiries. We found one or two of those here when we came.

There are no statistics to show the numbers of lapsed Catholics who return to the Church on their death-beds, nor those who return without waiting for death to summon them. One of the first visitors to the oratory at Doucegrove had not been to church for forty years, and I remember being amazed to see how quickly and completely her religion came back to her. She had not forgotten a word of it. There is an integrity in the deposit of Catholic truth which makes it able like gold to endure long burial, where inferior alloys would deteriorate and decay.

There are, of course, lapsed Catholics whom no missionary effort will reclaim, though these have not so much renounced their faith as allowed it to slip from them. Some of them do not know, or will not acknowledge, that it has slipped. "Of course, my church is the Brompton Oratory"— "I always go to the one o'clock Mass in Buenos

Ayres"—"Yes, Father, I'm going to Ramsgate for the day to-morrow and I'll get my Easter duties done there. I shouldn't dream of troubling you to hear my confession now." They are hardly ever defiant, nor will they ever allow anything to be said against Catholicism by their Protestant friends, but their determination to have nothing to do with the Church is shown by the almost heroic nature of their excuses for staying away.

However, the number of these is small in proportion to the number of those whose lapse is entirely due to circumstances, and who are at once restored when those circumstances are mended. The "leakage" exists, and from a human and psychological point of view must continue to exist. But it is not like the leak in a sinking ship, a thing which will spread and grow worse. It is, much of it, a temporary condition which the future will improve. The increase of man-power and of priest-power is bound to abate it. Though I have found Catholicism less dependent than Anglicanism on churches and clergy, it cannot by its very nature flourish without them, and it is a grave danger to faith for a Catholic to have to live for an indefinite period without the Sacraments. Directly there are enough priests to staff these remote country districts, either through the foundation of new parishes or the formation of mission centres, there is bound to be a decrease in the number of those who drift away on the winds of an alien culture.

A further encouragement is the thought of these Catholics who keep their faith in the face of every difficulty, spiritual and material. I know Catholic homes that are miles away from the nearest centre of Catholic life, which yet are Catholic homes in every good and true sense of the word, where the children are brought up in the faith, sent to Catholic schools (even at the cost of a daily 'bus ride of many miles) and brought to Mass every Sunday —father's old and struggling motor-bike coughing under its load of five immortal souls in their bodies. Such homes are more likely to restore the faith to England than all the gales of oratory and all the rivers of ink.

The Christian faith did not begin in churches and meeting-halls. It began in private houses. Mass was first said in Christian homes; and to-day, when the Mass is coming back to country districts from which it has been banished for nearly four hundred years, Christians meet "at the house of" so-

[247]

and-so, as long ago they met in Rome at the house of Clement or at the house of Pudentiana. . . . "Salute them that are of Jack Harman's household. . . . Salute Daisy and William Barnes and the church which is in their house . . . they who are of Little Doucegrove salute you. . . ."

When Mass was first said at Little Doucegrove, in the December of 1930, it was the first time that it had been said publicly in the neighbourhood since the Reformation. There is a local tradition, however, that in penal times it was said secretly at Tufton (originally Tuktone) Place, about a mile from Northiam; and the tradition is borne out by one of the local place-names, Superstition Corner, which, though it has never been exactly fixed, belongs most probably to the cross-roads nearest the reputed mass-house.

On this legend I based the first of my two Catholic novels. *Superstition Corner* was originally conceived as the title of an immense book which should give the story of the neighbourhood from the banishment of the Mass in 1559 down to the return of the Mass in 1930. The story should not be only religious, but historical and social as well; I would show the changes even of the place-names, transforming Glaseney into Glasseye, Ferdinglonde into Farthing Lane, Piramannys Garden into Perryman's Cross, and so on as the book advanced. I would also show the history of my own home, tracing its foundation to Robert Douce, the Frenchman who came in the sixteenth century to teach Sussex iron-workers the newest French methods of smelting iron.

But when I had finished the first part of the book I was not satisfied with it and put it aside while I wrote *The Ploughman's Progress*, a novel dealing with agricultural conditions during the national slump through which we were passing at the time. I wrote it entirely from the outside. It is a patchwork of local events and observations, held together by my indignation that England should in such a manner throw the best of herself away. Living in the country all the year round, I was seeing every day how the spirit of the town is crushing out the life of the country-side, so that the men who for centuries have lived both in and on the fields are faced with the choice either of seeking work in the towns or with those who come into the country from the towns, or of staying where they are as vagrants, robbed of their homes, robbed of their skill, unwanted in a country of canned and imported foodstuffs, ignored by one political party, crushed by the other. The old nursery battle between Platnix Farm and "the ugly houses guarded by city red" had been a forecast of the battle now being waged up and down England by the forces of the country and the town—and this time Platnix is not likely to win.

The book is also a sort of half-hearted sequel to *The End of the House of Alard*. The Alards in their early days had been the protagonists of *Superstition Corner*, and when I had finished with them in modern times I went back to where I had left them in the sixteenth century. I had, however, lost my appetite for the stupendous. If I wrote a history of the neighbourhood, it should be in digestible parts. On re-reading *Superstition Corner* I found that I liked it better than when I had put it aside, better than I had expected. It seemed to have about it the "gleam" of my very earliest books, as if in seeing the country-side divested of the bungalows and filling-stations of adult experience, I had gone back to Platnix Farm again. To write it I had soaked myself in pre-Shakespearean plays, and about these, too, there is an aqueous clearness which belongs only to the landscapes of childhood. I did not expect *Superstition Corner* to be a success, for I knew the troubles attached to an historical novel only sixty thousand words long, but it gave me more artistic satisfaction than anything I had written since *Green Apple Harvest*.

It is certainly a better book than *Gallybird*, the second part of my original novel, which was published only six months after *Superstition Corner*, and carries on the history of the Alards and Douces into the seventeenth century. The district was at this time full of Huguenot refugees, and I might have spread my story very much more widely than I did in the origins of many local families. The novel, indeed, though full length, suffers from over-compression. It might have made a really fine book of a hundred and fifty thousand words; as it is, the narrative moves so quickly that it comes perilously near a yarn. I do not know why I never thought of making it longer. I could have done much more with the characters, too, if I had. There are some promising sketches, but they all want filling in. If ever I should follow George Moore's advice . . . but that is not likely.

Neither do I suppose that I shall ever finish my history of the Alards. Even at the moment of its conception the later episodes were rather dim, and now they have almost faded out of my mind. Here pictures succeed one another so rapidly that it is difficult for me to be faithful long to any single one of them. I do not seem to have any facilities for mental cold storage. It is true that I have been able to revive work that has been for some reason put aside, but already that work has acquired enough shape and substance of its own to constitute an independent existence. I doubt if I could ever revive an abandoned idea.

These two historical novels were, apart from their position as parts of a more important whole, an effort to solve the difficulties I had met in my work ever since I lost the faculty of writing from unconscious reactions. To withdraw into a far-back century, which nothing of myself had ever touched save my imagination, seemed as good a way as any of dealing with that fatal tendency to "think." My mind was safely occupied with objective details and made no attempt to interfere with the characters and story.

The drawback here is that I am too objective,

too detached. There is no longer that connection between my self and my work which was obvious in those earlier novels where my personality was least intrusive. The god is no longer both immanent and transcendent; he is as detached from his creation as any First Cause of a Victorian biologist. As a result something vital is missing. *Superstition Corner* may please me artistically, but it does not satisfy me personally. *Gallybird* might be somebody else's story.

A better way of getting over the difficulty was my revival of childhood's days in *The Children's Summer* and *Selina is Older*, published respectively in 1933 and 1935. Neither of these is quite plain fact or quite pure fiction. Imagination has gilded memory—attractively, to judge by the reception of both books. Within their narrow limits they solve my problem, for both are written from a full consciousness, and yet in neither is there any intrusive "thinking." The trouble is that the limits are so narrow. The pleasure of this imaginative reconstruction is great, and there is nothing I should like better than to write the whole of my life this way—fiction stepping in where fact is wanting in effectiveness or grace. But it is not a trick—for it is

[253]

a trick—that can be repeated indefinitely; it would soon become mechanical, and I should find myself the parent of yet another Victorian universe.

I have hope of a solution on different lines. Though *Rose Deeprose* (published in 1936) did not win the favour of the critics in England (and perhaps it might have compromised with *Gallybird* in the matter of length, giving its predecessor some forty thousand words), it shows, I think, a method of literary construction which could be carried further with advantage. There is no point in comparing it with *Sussex Gorse* or *Joanna Godden*, as these two novels belong to a literary phase I have left behind, and to which there can be no return. The true comparison lies between *Rose Deeprose* and *Shepherds in Sackcloth* or *The Ploughman's Progress*. In those earlier books I have taken whole episodes in chunks from life, and many of the characters are portraits showing, as portraits often do when the artist has only just started portrait-painting, too great a consciousness of the model. *Rose Deeprose* is equally from life, but not so identifiably. The particles have been better digested, or rather, to change the simile, the material is not taken out in patches but pulled out in threads

[254]

which are woven together unrecognizably into a new stuff. I do not suppose that I shall ever again write from the secret storehouse of my unconscious mind, but the whole of life outside should be rich enough to give me all I need, once I have learned how to use it.

I have to learn a new method of writing, just as I have to learn a new method of religion. In religion I have to learn to look not outwards but inwards, and in my writing I have to learn to look not inwards but outwards. Before I became a Catholic my religion was largely concerned with external observances, with services, ritual and beauty; now I have to do without much that I used to consider essential, and worship in a manner more closely akin to Little Bethel than I should have thought edifying ten years ago. When I began to write I could find within myself all the material I needed, bright with the star-dust with which the unconscious gilds even the dullest gingerbread; now I have to resign myself to the fact that the cupboard of this internal Mother Hubbard is bare, and I must take my imagination out into the highways.

Actually the change in my writing has been

more fundamental than the change in my religion, but it is less obvious because there is here no change in externals. I still write about Sussex and shall probably continue to write about Sussex—the setting of *Rose Deeprose* in the Kentish weald means nothing at all, for East Sussex is far more like West Kent than it is like West Sussex. But even Sussex has suffered a change, and my feeling for it has become far more detached and external, and at the same time more detailed and intimate, than it used to be in the days when I lived in the town and the country northward of Brede was just a rare and glorious adventure. Living in the midst of it, sharing its life, its farms and fields a part of everyday experience, I can no longer see it in the same shining light as when it was for me excitement, holiday, wish and dream. But I am more than ever dependent on absolute familiarity with my background if I am to move my creatures freely against it, having lost that "uncanny second self" which was once able to take me more or less successfully to Yucatan.

I am not unlike a person who having for years played the piano by ear is now for the first time learning to read music. It is a slow process, and one is even handicapped by one's earlier capacity—one would probably do better if one had never played at all. I find my fingers stumbling on the keys and the connection between eye and hand is not perfectly established, so that the performance at times is laboured and lacking in inspiration. But I persevere with it because I know that the best music comes from the brain and is the result of a deliberate intellectual process. The great composers worked like mathematicians rather than the entranced mediums of popular imagination, and I refuse to believe that art is in its essence so neurotic that it cannot be successfully produced by a unified personality but requires for the best results some psychological immaturity or even a lesion of consciousness.

In time I may come to a fusion of the old and the new methods. It would be ideal, of course, if thought and instinct, conscious and unconscious, could become allied here as they have become allied in the religious field. And here again my Sussex background helps me; for I am aware that though it too has become an affair of external knowledge and experience rather than of intuition, there are roots going down from that surface, deep down,

very deep down, into the deepest secrets of the unconscious first-born. Crit Hall and Platnix are not
so very far away in the dimension of space—only a
few miles north and south; some day I may find
that they are just as near in the dimension of time,
and the years may take me back to them as easily
as the miles.

Composed in Linotype Janson
Format by A. W. Rushmore
Manufactured by The Haddon Craftsmen
Published by HARPER & BROTHERS, *New York and London*

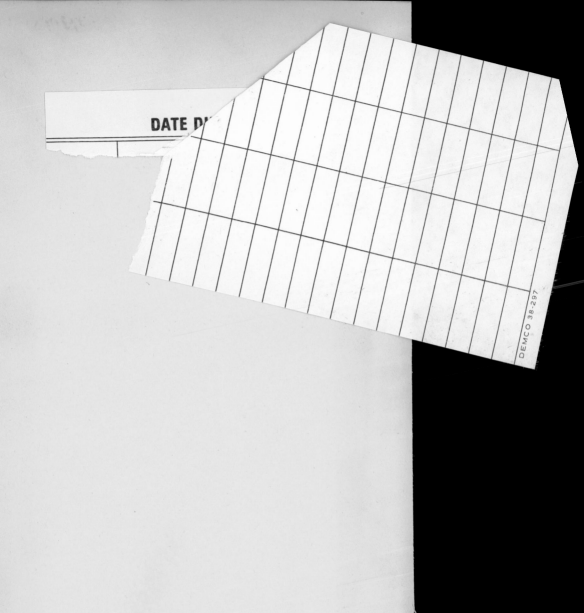

DATE D